Bitter, Party of One...

Your Table is Ready

1st in a series of Bitter Books.

www.bitterbooks.com

Bitter, Party of One...
Your Table is Ready

Relationship advice from a guy
who has no business giving it.

7/30/05

Larry Star

Dear Luann & Brue,
Thanks for laughing at me!
ATTEN-HUT!

iUniverse, Inc.
New York Lincoln Shanghai

Bitter, Party of One... Your Table is Ready
Relationship advice from a guy who has
no business giving it.

iUniverse books may be ordered through booksellers or by contacting:

iUniverse
2021 Pine Lake Road, Suite 100
Lincoln, NE 68512
www.iuniverse.com
1-800-Authors (1-800-288-4677)

ISBN-13: 978-0-595-35692-8 (pbk)
ISBN-13: 978-0-595-80170-1 (ebk)
ISBN-10: 0-595-35692-3 (pbk)
ISBN-10: 0-595-80170-6 (ebk)

Printed in the United States of America

Image Credits
        Cover photo: Brandon Hildebrand/HildeDesigns.com
        Cover concept: Larry Star
        Bio photo: Dorothy Pierce/Just Moments Ago…portraits by doe
        Illustration: Wes Shreffler/Tetan Design

Any similarity to any of the chicks I've married, dated, hung out with, or known, may, or may not, be purely coincidental. If you think any of these stories resemble you or something you've done and are very pissed off about it being included in this book, tough shit. Life goes on. At least you have something to tell your grandkids.

All content herein is satire and should be taken in a humorous light. If you find it hits too close to home, give me your number so we can commiserate over a beer at the nudie bar.

Do not try any of this at home.

Not responsible for mental breakdowns.

Not intended for children under 43 years of age.

Not for ophthalmic use.

Microwaveable.

For Alicia

Husbands, love your wives, and be not bitter against them.

~*The Bible; Colossians 3:19*

Yeah. Sure. Like that'll happen.

~*Larry Star*

CONTENTS

PREFACE

Hello there.

First, let me thank you for buying this book. Even if you didn't buy it, I want to thank you for looking at it.

You may, or may not, know who I am. I'm betting it's one of the two. Actually, there is a third possibility: You could be one of those people who *think* they don't know who I am until they realize I am eBay's infamous Wedding Dress Guy. And yes, that's me on the cover of this book.

For those of you who *really* don't know who I am, I'm just a regular guy, with a regular job, who tried to sell my ex's wedding dress online. I'm not a spiteful person, just practical. I decided to put the dress up for auction to get a little cash, some baseball tickets, and possibly, a few laughs from my friends. I wrote the most derisively funny ad copy I could think of describing the once-worn wedding dress, but I also did something else a bit non-conventional—I actually wore it for the photos.

Well, the auction for the dress with my somewhat bitter, misogynistic—yet descriptive—copy took off like wildfire. The media got wind of it and I appeared on numerous news TV shows, radio programs, and magazines. I even did a stint as a stand up comic. For almost six months I was a so-called "media darling."

In the five short days from the initial posting on eBay, the details of my failed marriage and my slant on life were avidly viewed in cubicles by hundreds of thousands of employees who, instead, should have been doing real work on their computers.

Corporate productivity continued to slide while those same employees e-mailed me their comments on the auction.

In those e-mails, some people called me a cult hero; some people called me an asshole. I like to think that I, like all other regular guys, fall somewhere in between. (Oh, I may lean towards the asshole side, but at least I'm loveable. No, really.) But, a majority of those e-mails thanked me for the laugh I gave them.

What's more, in all the positive e-mails I have received, half asked me for relationship advice. The other half asked me to write a book based on my auction, my musings, or my life. I have decided to combine everything, thus resulting in the pearl of wisdom you now hold.

So, again, if you bought this book, I give you my utmost appreciation. If you didn't, please do so immediately, because I really hate my freaking day job. I would much rather write for you for a living.

~Larry Star

The original eBay auction was preserved in its entirety and can be seen on-line at: http://weddingdressguy.com/original_ebay_ad/ebaylisting.html

Larry can be contacted at larry@weddingdressguy.com

INTRODUCTION

The only thing to do with good advice is pass it on. It is never any use to oneself.

~Oscar Wilde

ADViCe On ADViCe

Advice. A six-lettered word, advice is many things. It can be light. It can be heavy. It can be soothing or painful. It is something people can treasure and learn from—or something they can mock. It is endured, asked about, scoffed at, indulged in, and spat out. Good, bad, or indifferent, advice is what makes the world go 'round.

It seems that everyone at some point in his or her life gets advice, but, more often than not, it is given when it wasn't even asked for.

Sometimes, the advice given is welcome: "Your ass looks absolutely fantabulous in those culottes! I think you should buy them."

Sometimes, it is not: "From where I'm sitting, you don't really need that third helping of cheesecake."

Sometimes, the advice is disguised as a compliment: "You make the *best* steaks. Go start the grill and I'll take care of everything else."

Sometimes, it's as blunt as the head it's trying to enter: "Everything you cook tastes like crap. Just go make the steaks, and try not to screw it up."

Good advice is a scarce commodity; bad advice is omnipresent. Even worse, bad advice always sounds good, or, at the very least, plausible, which is what could make it so dangerous.

But, perhaps, the ultimate danger is that bad advice is always easier to follow than good advice. For example:

Good advice: Take an aspirin once a day. It's good for the heart.

Or: Open a Roth IRA.

Or: Eat lots of fiber. It's good for the bowels.

Bad advice: Wireless communication is a fad. Stick with the old Trimline.

Or: You're on a protein diet? Dude—that means carte blanche on the bacon!

Or: Don't waste those tickets to *Women's Tag Team Mud Wrestling Extravaganza XVI* at the fairgrounds. Just go. No one wants to go to a boring old funeral, anyway.

In the forthcoming pages you will ~~suffer~~ go through an entire relationship with me. After every episode, I'll share a valuable lesson, which that particular event taught me. Whether or not the lesson I learned is actually *good* advice is entirely up to you.

IN THE BEGINNING

Gravitation is not responsible for people falling in love.

~Albert Einstein

Cheeseburger In Paradise

"Hey, how *you* doin'?" This pop-culture phrase, in one form or another, flashes through the mind of virtually every red-blooded American male whenever he sees an attractive woman, regardless of his marital/relationship status. Sucking your teeth, while eyeing the woman up and down, is optional. It's a rare instance when a man can actually verbalize this phrase and not come out looking like the boorish pig virtually every red-blooded American female thinks he is.

Case in point: One day during lunch I was sitting in my favorite eatery, masticating my favorite pastrami-topped cheeseburger, when this unbelievably attractive brunette sat down at the table next to me (I say "unbelievably" because to this day I can't believe I thought she was even remotely attractive. But, I was coming off a break-up three weeks prior and was feeling a little, uh, lonely…).

She was dressed in navy blue slacks with a matching blazer offset by a white blouse. She had the kind of hair that looked like she spent hours on in the morning getting it just so. And she had pink nails. Pink nails. Pepto-Bismol pink nails.

I noticed she kept looking at her watch and then at the door like she was waiting for someone.

With Batman-like deductive reasoning, I knew she would not be sitting there alone much longer. I knew my window of opportunity for meeting this girl was closing rapidly. I knew I had to say something, and say it fast.

I leaned in. "Hey, how *you* doin'?"

She turned to me. "Excuse me?"

It was then that I realized I was clutching my favorite pastrami-topped cheeseburger with both hands, literally squeezing dollops of ketchup and beef fat into my lap, and my cheeks looked like I had just crammed two baseballs in my mouth. What I thought came out as "Hey, how you doin'?" actually came out as "Heomunoonin."

I started coughing. Uncontrollably.

"Are you all right?" She seemed concerned.

Cough "Umaw—" *cough* "winethan—" *cough* "fanyoo—" *cough.*

She helped me stand up and patted me on the back. She got me some water. With my hand gestures I assured her I was fine and didn't need the Heimlich maneuver. She was really cute and helpful. And she didn't mind the little chunks of pastrami and cheese I managed to spit on her suit. "That's why they make drycleaners," she said.

Ψ

Lesson Learned

Don't ever be afraid to be yourself. If she won't love you for who you are now, she sure as hell won't love you for who you will become later. The bottom line is you need to love you for who you are now because you won't even recognize yourself after she gets through with you.

NO Insight In Sight, Just Bull

I was sitting on the edge of my bed looking at the phone number she had given me. It was written on the napkin I used to wipe off the food particles I inadvertently spit on her. Actually, I didn't wipe them off; I kind of smeared them on her blazer and embedded them into threads. We exchanged numbers so I could take care of the dry cleaning bill. But, I couldn't help but think there was some sort of spark there. The way she looked at me, the concern in her voice, the way she slapped away my hands as I tried to clean her suit. Yes, there was definitely something there.

All the advice columns say to wait the customary three days before you call. Well, I'm here to tell you that that is just hogwash. If you meet someone and you like her, go ahead and call. Just don't make a pest of yourself.

So, there I was, eleven hours later, looking at her number on the napkin, waffling about calling her.

You know, I decided for once in my life, I was going to take the bull by the horns. I was going to call her. Screw the advice columns. So what, it was midnight? So what, it was Monday night? So what, I had to be up at 5 a.m.?

Wait. I was being selfish. She probably had to be up early as well. She looked like a businesswoman, someone who'd actually have a job. Not like Miss I'm-gonna-sit-on-my-ass-all-day-and-watch-Jerry-Springer, my last girlfriend.

That woman was the laziest girl I ever had the misfortune to date. I wasn't quite sure if her laziness sprang from her drinking or from her smoking. Which, when I thought about it, brought up the nagging ponderable: Did she drink and smoke because she was broke, or was she broke because she drank and smoked?

She would let the garbage pile up because she thought recycling meant she had to pedal somewhere. She couldn't wait for me to come over so I could look for the remote she misplaced. And her eating habits were that of, well—a guy. She thought PB&J was pizza, beer and junk food. Come to think of it, that was her only redeeming quality.

Well, enough of that. Back to the matter at hand: Should I call the number on the napkin? You know, after thinking about Miss Springer-phile, and what that relationship turned into, I thought I would just let the proverbial bull go his own way.

So, Miss Businesswoman-with-the-pink-nails, you'll just have to wait the customary three days before I call you.

I am just too tired to find your remote.

Ψ

<u>*Lesson Learned*</u>

If you stay up late arguing with yourself, eventually you will lose. Get used to it.

Daydream Believer

I was so excited.

I walked into the restaurant and asked the maitre d' if my table was ready. He informed me that it was and my party was already seated.

He showed me to the table and there she sat. She was wearing a skirt and her legs were crossed. She stood up to greet me. *Wow. Nice legs.*

I extended my hand. "Hi, it's very nice to see you again. I have your money here for the dry cleaning of your suit." I patted my pocket. "Let's sit down, shall we," I added as I pushed her chair in for her. *So far, so good, Mr. Suave.*

She thanked me.

"Thanks for agreeing to have dinner with me. I just wanted to make up for spitting all over you the other day."...*like the freaking idiot I am, and I hope you never see that side of me again.*

"Well, it was hard to say no considering how persistent you were."

"Was I really? I'm sorry. I just didn't want you to think I was a complete boor. I wanted a second chance to talk with you under better circumstances." *Great. She thinks I'm pushy. Strike one.*

"I must say this certainly is under better circumstances," she said as she looked around. "This place is very nice. I've always wanted to come here but I've never had the chance."

"My pleasure, I assure you." I picked up the menu. *Ok, redemption. She likes my choice of restaurant.*

"Go ahead, have anything you want," I said. *Just don't pick the most expensive thing, ok? I'm not made of money, you know.*

"Well, you know, everything just looks so good. I can't decide if I want steak or seafood."

"Go ahead and get both. Get the surf and turf. That sounds really good, actually. I may get that myself." *Sheesh! Will ya look at the price? Please don't pick the surf and turf…please don't pick the surf and turf…*

"That sounds terrific. I'll have that, rare, with a Caesar salad on the side, and a glass of cabernet."

"Good choice," I smiled. "I'll have the same." *Great. She picked the surf and turf. Now I have to get it, too. This is going to cost a fortune. There goes my bill money.*

When the waiter came, I ordered for the both of us.

"So, were you born and raised here?" I asked. *We might as well get the conversation rolling, ok?*

"I was born in Corpus Christi, but we moved here when I was four. Oh, here is a funny story. When I was seven, I went to…"

Boy, she has the nicest lips. I wonder how she kisses. I bet she kisses great. She has a nice smile, too. Straight white teeth, and a cute dimple on her right cheek. She sure is a lot cuter than I remembered, although it's only been a few days since I met her. I hope I don't blow it. I sure like this one.

"…and it swelled up to the size of a tennis ball." She laughed at her story.

What the hell did she just say? I hope she doesn't ask me. Let me change the subject.

I quickly asked her, "Do you like sports?" *Maybe I should listen to her answer this time.*

"I like to watch figure skating. I think it's just so beautiful…"

I bet she doesn't like football. I never really met a woman that did. Actually, that's not true. I've met several women who did but they all had facial hair and smoked cigars.

"…graceful when I was a teen. How about you? You look like you are pretty athletic. Do you play much sports?"

Ok, now it's getting thick in here. She is either blind or very patronizing, but I'll play along.

"When I was younger I used to lift weights. My upper body was in the shape of a 'V'. Now it's just in the shape of an 'O'." *I'll charm her with wit.*

She laughed. *That's a good sign. I sure would like to see her again. But what's up with those pink nails?*

After we had our dessert, the waiter came by and set a gilded billfold down on the table.

It was time to pay.

Holy crap! That's not a check; it's a collection letter. Maybe I can make payment arrangements.

The night went on and I tried to make a point of asking her questions to see if we were compatible or not. I also tried not to monopolize the conversation, although it wasn't that difficult. She didn't need a lot of prompting to talk. This might wear on me later, but for now, it's cute.

Here is the breakdown: Doesn't like football, trucks, auto-racing, or motorcycles. Doesn't eat too much fried foods, chips, red meat, or commercial breakfast cereal. She seems highly opinionated about politics, music and fashion. Likes pink.

What we have in common: Zero.

"Thanks for a really pleasant evening, Larry."

"You're entirely welcome. You know, I really think we have so much in common. I would love to see you again. Could we make plans for next Saturday night?"

"I think I'm free. Call me during the week."

Woohoo! I'm in!

Ψ

<u>*Lesson Learned*</u>

What we have here is the right-brain, bottom-brain syndrome. Your right-brain is telling you that she isn't that much of a good fit with you, yet your bottom-brain tells you she would look really good naked. If you stood on your head so your bottom-brain was really your top-brain, you might see everything with more clarity. Of course, this is only a theory, because if you were to actually stand on your head, you would be trying to look up her skirt.

creameD

It's amazing what happens to your vision when you meet someone new. When I was with Miss I'm-sitting-on-my-butt-all-damn-day, cleaning the apartment was not a priority. She never cared if it was clean, dirty, cluttered, dusty, on fire—it just didn't matter to her as long as she had the remote, some Keebler Swiss Fudgies, a pack of smokes, and a bottle of beer with a straw. Consequently, I didn't care either.

Once she was out of my life I gradually took back control of my house. I started tidying up the place. I actually put dirty clothes in the hamper and not on the bicycle. I started using real dishes again, not just the box that the pizza came in. And I went on a killing rampage, slaughtering every damn dust bunny I could find.

But my sense of house cleaning reached its pinnacle when I invited my new pink-nailed date to my place for the first time. I began to see my apartment not as the hip, inviting, swinging-cool bachelor pad I always thought it was, but as the industrial frat house it *really* was.

I knew I needed to crank up the cleanliness wattage when I went into the bathroom and really saw it for the first time. I never knew that I had carpeting in the bathroom. This is what I mean by your vision becoming more acute, because under careful inspection I realized it wasn't carpeting: it was hair.

My date was coming over to my house in three hours for a nice cozy romantic evening, complete with candlelit dinner, and there I was in the bathroom on my knees ripping up sheets of hair. Where the hell did this freaking hair come from anyway? My ex-girlfriend never bathed, so that couldn't be it. She would have had to have actually gotten up off her fat ass and touched water. Come to think of it, I couldn't recall her ever going to the bathroom at all. Hmmm. Note to self: Buy new couch.

Then it dawned on me—this was *my* hair! What the hell happens to a guy in his thirties? Some kind of genetic metamorphosis takes place where hair starts sprouting up all over his body in places he had never thought would. I mean, young guys see these old men with hair that goes from their ears to their feet and never give any thought that one day they, too, will look like Paulie from Rocky.

I remember the first time I saw a hair sprout on my shoulder; I thought I was turning into The Fly. Did I ever heed the warning signs? No, I did not. I never took care of it. I never even thought that if there were one, there would be more. It didn't occur to me that one little hair would bring his friends and colonize my back like a bunch of curly pilgrims.

I stood up, took my shirt off and looked in the mirror. I was mortified. The guy staring back at me with the horrified look was wearing a brunette sweater.

If I'd wanted to have sex tonight, I knew I had better take care of this. I looked at my watch. In two and a half hours, she would be here. I put my shirt on and ran out of the apartment to the nearest drug store.

Little did I know the embarrassment that would ensue. I approached the pharmacist. "Excuse me, um, where can I find the defibrillating cream?"

"The what?" she responded

"The defibrillating cream. You know, the, uh, hair removal stuff. It's, uh, for my wife. For my wife's legs." I wiped my forehead with my sleeve.

"Oh," she giggled. "You mean the depilatory cream. That would be in aisle two, on the left about half-way down."

"Thanks."

Great. She must've thought I was an idiot. Either that, or some medical wunderkind with hairy ventricles.

I bought three bottles of the stuff and went back home.

I looked at the bathroom, with half of its carpet missing and I panicked. There was no way I was going to be done in time, but I had to try.

I took off my shirt and opened the bottle. Boy, did this stuff stink. Stink, yes, but it had to be done.

I spun around the room dumbfounded. What the hell was I going to put it on with? Women use this stuff for their legs. *They* can reach their legs (well, some of them can). I *can't* reach my back. What the hell was I going to do?

Then I had the brilliant idea to stand in the hairy tub (just noticed that, too, by the way), squeeze it out on the tiled wall and put my back into the goo. I must have been some sight—standing half-naked in a bathtub, with my arms outstretched, slithering my back on the wall, like some sort of Jesus Jell-O mold.

When I was satisfied I had gotten this stuff into every pore, I got out of the tub. It was then that I decided, much like every other man who has ever used a woman's product, to read the directions.

It clearly stated, "Test a small area of your skin. Do not leave on longer than 10 minutes. May cause redness or burning to sensitive skin. Consult a physician if redness or burning persists." It's funny how you don't notice the pain until you read something that says you may experience it.

My back was on freaking fire! They should have called this stuff "Follicle Napalm." I looked at my back in the mirror. The cream was starting to harden and crack, and the short curly hairs were now straight and roughly two inches long.

It was stinging so badly, I had to get it off. The bottle said to use a damp towel at first, then lukewarm water to clean up the rest. It's really tough when your arms just don't bend that way. It took two towels and a twenty-minute cold shower to get all the cream off my back.

I have to say that the cold water really soothed me. It soothed me enough to realize that I only had an hour left to clean the bathroom and that I had just taken a shower with my pants and shoes on.

I spent most of that remaining hour cleaning the bathtub and wall from the hair removal goo and peeling up the rest of the hair carpet.

Later that evening we were lying on the couch, kissing, just as I had hoped. I was holding her and she was stroking my hair. Hair, which by the way, started to come out in clumps. Apparently, it hadn't occurred to me to use a shower cap when I did the Nair Tango.

Ψ

Lesson Learned

When trying out a new grooming regimen, be sure to have the proper instruments, a dry run through, and plenty of time. Otherwise, your efforts may go right down the drain.

Propinkwity

Do you remember meeting that special someone? Do you remember how you couldn't wait to see that person? Do you remember going on a date when everything had to be just right? Do you remember thinking you were gonna get some?

It was our third date. You know what they say: The third time's the charm.

Everyone always remembers the first time they have sex with someone, no matter how awkward it is. Even though the tenth or twentieth time is infinitely better because all of the inhibitions are gone and you know each other's bodies and reactions, people only seem remember the first time.

With me it was no different.

I had a feeling we were going to wind up horizontal after the date. There were little things I picked up on during our last date, which told me perhaps she would be willing to take the plunge, so to speak. Like when she said, "No, honey, I'm not ready, yet."

The operative word there is *yet*.

Yet.

Yet infers eventuality.

Yet is also an extremely close cousin of *yes*.

As a matter of fact, the difference between the two is only one letter. Just think of it—one tiny little letter away from us getting naked. See? We men focus on the positive. We don't focus on the *no*, only on the *yet* and its jubilant little cousin who wants to see us get naked.

For this particular date, she was to come to my house, and then we'd go out from there.

I made reservations at a fine steakhouse, not unlike the place we had our first date (see the chapter titled *Daydream Believer*). This time it was a restaurant that I delivered to, so the manager knew me by name. This would impress her.

I also got us tickets to a play at the local repertory. They were performing *Bob & Carol & Ted & Alice*.

Afterwards, she would come back to my place for a nightcap, or maybe even a movie. Then, that's precisely when I thought the evening would really start smoking.

I groomed myself, got dressed and went through my checklist:

A bottle of wine—check.

A new red light bulb with dimmer—check.

Both, 9½ Weeks and Wild Orchid—check.

A can of whip cream—check.

A fresh tray of ice cubes—check.

A candle and some matches—check.

A box of condoms—check.

I had wanted to get some oysters, but the local mini-mart didn't have any. So, I bought a box of Oysterettes instead.

I wanted everything to be just right to put her in the mood.

I bought a new set of sheets, in case she wanted to do it in the bed. I steam cleaned the carpets, in case she wanted to do it on the floor. I bought new place mats, in case she wanted to do it on the kitchen table.

I even bought new underwear.

Ding-dong.

The bell. There she was. I couldn't wait to feel her pink nails scratching the hell out of my newly hair-free back from her utter ecstasy.

I opened the door. "Hello, baby!"

It wasn't her. Instead, it was my worst nightmare.

It was Miss Springer-phile. She was holding a cigarette in one hand and a can with a paper sack wrapped around it with the other. You didn't have to be a rocket surgeon to know that that was a can of Colt .45. And it was aimed right at me.

"Well, don't you look snazzy," she said.

"I wish I could say the same."

She was dressed in gray sweatpants that were apparently a tad too small, which made her look a tad too big, a torn Budweiser t-shirt (which looked a hell of a lot like the one I was missing immediately after she left), and she wore a pink bandana. Not Pepto-Bismol pink, but pink nonetheless.

"I've dressed up for you before," she said.

"What? When did you ever dress up for me? Oh, yeah, I forgot. You had that lovely threadbare Muumuu you wore on Saturday nights."

Then I added, "And, can you not smoke in the hall, please?"

"It's just a cigarette, it won't kill you."

She sounded like she was just one node away from a tracheotomy.

"That's not the point," I said. "This is a non-smoking building, remember?"

"Alright, alright." She dropped the cigarette on the floor and extinguished it with her filthy sneaker. Real classy.

Speaking of classy, I thought about my date and I started to panic.

How embarrassing would that have been if my new love interest met my ex-girlfriend? I was in the showing-off stage of our new relationship. I couldn't have my new date think I ever had sex with this semblance of a woman standing before me. I would never get a fourth date.

"What the hell are you doing here, anyway?" I asked her as I was looking beyond her hoping my date wouldn't come up the hall behind her.

"I just came for the rest of my things." Her eyes seemed glassy.

"I haven't seen you in almost two months and you choose tonight to come and get your crap? Couldn't you have called first?"

"I couldn't. You changed your number," she replied.

"Oh, yeah. Well, that's because I didn't want you calling me. Listen, you need to leave right now, ok?"

"Not without my stuff." She wiped her nose with the back of her hand.

"What stuff? You didn't own anything. If you mean your beer label collection, I threw it out."

I looked down the hall, again, and then at her. "Come on, I'll give your stuff to you later. You really need to leave right now."

I felt like I was going to get fleas just talking to her. It's amazing to me that I actually slept with her. Then again, she did bring the beer…

"I want my clothes and my Walkman." She seemed adamant.

I looked at my watch, and said, "Ok, ok. I'll get them. Stay right here."

I ran into the bedroom and got the box of her things from the closet that I set aside, and then went into the bathroom.

I was cutting it close. My date would be here any minute.

I grabbed a pail from under the sink and dumped her crap into it. Then I ran back to the door where she was waiting with half-closed eyelids.

"Here you go," I said as I handed her the pail. "Now could you leave, please?"

"Thank you very much." I think she tried to say that with as much dignity as she could.

She turned and started walking back down the hall, just as my date was walking up.

Oh shit.

But, all the worrying was for naught, as they passed each other in the hall without saying a word.

I gave my honey a kiss.

"Who was that?" she asked.

"Who was who?"

"That woman coming from your apartment."

"Oh, she was just the cleaning lady. Come on in."

I waited a little while before we left, to make sure that my ex was gone, which she was.

There. Bullet dodged. This was good. It was an omen of things to come.

The rest of the evening went almost entirely as I had planned. With my charm and humor, and a little help from the theatre troupe and Mickey Rourke, I managed to seduce this pink-nailed vixen. She wound up right where I wanted her—in my bed. And damn near naked, to boot.

As she slid in bed she exclaimed, "Oh, new sheets, huh? I love the feel of new sheets."

"And I love the feel of you," I said with as much suaveness as I could.

We kissed passionately for a while and she started moving down. She removed my underwear and started to kiss my nether regions.

After a few moments, she started clearing her throat as if she were trying to bring up a hairball. That's definitely not the most romantic sound in the world.

She tried to spit out something that was obviously lodged deep in her throat. After about two minutes of her hacking she finally dislodged the foreign matter and spat it on the bed.

"What happened, baby?" I asked.

"I don't know, honey," she said as she reached for the tiny white object that was spat out.

I leaned in close to her to see what it was.

It was paper tag that said: *Inspected by No. 52.*

Ψ

<u>*Lesson Learned*</u>

I am now a proponent for disclaimers on underwear packages: *Please wash before use. Serious injury or death may occur.*

DATING

Happiness is having a large, loving, caring, close-knit family in another city.

~George Burns

The Beach Is Back

One of the things we each liked to do in the summer was go to the beach. This might've seemed like a really cool thing to do together on the surface, but there were logistics to be worked out.

For instance, she likes to bring a cooler filled with White Zinfandel and wine glasses, brie and crackers, and some carrots and celery sticks with ranch dressing. She also brings blankets, an umbrella, a change of clothes, a change of shoes, a camera, two pairs of glasses, a reflector, suntan lotion *and* sunscreen, a straw hat, the odd hair clippie thing and scrunchie, a small make-up case (small is a relative term here), a book, magazines, and a radio. All of those items needed to be prepared, carried, loaded into the vehicle, unloaded, and carried to the destination with the process repeating for the return trip.

I, on the other hand, like to ride my motorcycle to the beach. I strap a towel to the seat and go. Needless to say, this posed a bit of a problem.

The first time we went to the beach together, I did the gentlemanly thing and succumbed to her wishes, taking everything aforementioned; I even cut up the carrots and celery. I picked up the cooler and put it in her car. I grabbed the bag of clothes and shoes, and put it in her car. I carried the blankets and towels and put them in her car. I gathered the books, magazines, camera and radio and put them in her car. I could have used a little help with the make-up case, but I eventually got it to within ten feet of her car. I dragged it the rest of the way, waited five minutes to catch my breath, and then bench-pressed it into the trunk. *Vasili Alexeyev has got nothin' on me.*

I turned to look for my honey. There she was in the driver's seat with the car running, the air conditioner on, the visor down, and her face plastered against the mirror. I couldn't really tell what she was doing, but it looked like she was reaming out her eye socket with the fingernail of her pinky. It's a familiar sight, though usually seen on the freeway during the morning commute. Any female—regardless of age, size, class, or financial stature—will, at any given time, be up to her respective knuckle in eyeball. I often wonder if that was some sort of rite of passage; something that their mothers taught them just like dads teach their sons how to whistle with both index fingers stuffed in their mouth.

I closed the trunk lid, wiped my sweating brow with my forearm and thought that maybe she should invest in a minivan. You know, something with a low lift-over height to eliminate hernias.

I walked around to the side of the car, opened the passenger door and clambered in.

"What took you so long?" she asked with her pinky still excavating her optical cavity. "I was hoping to get a really good spot before it got crowded."

"Sorry, baby. I just had to run back inside for a second to take some ibuprofen for my back, that's all. I think I may have pulled it with the last bag."

I took a breath and added, "Ok, sweets, we're loaded—hit it!" I smiled, tapped the dashboard and waited.

And waited.

And waited.

I leaned in, "Uh, the car's all loaded now. We can go."

"Ok, honey, just a second," she said, still polishing her cornea.

Meanwhile, since it was 90 degrees outside and the air-conditioning was on full blast inside, frost started to form on the windows and I was starting to get the beginnings of frostbite.

"Honey, I thought you said you didn't want to get there too late so we could get good spot," I queried, trying not to show any sign of shivering in my voice.

"Ok, dear, I'm ready now." She flipped up the visor, put the car in gear and we were off.

We got there about twenty minutes later with only three or four comments on how she needs to bring the car in to get the air-conditioning checked; it didn't blow cold enough for her liking. It did, however, take us another twenty minutes to find a parking spot within walking distance of the beach. This reaffirmed my always wanting to take my motorcycle.

"Uh, babe? How are we going to get all this stuff to the beach? It's a three block walk."

"Well, I figure we can take some things now, find our spot and then we could go back and get the rest of it," she answered.

"We, huh?" I muttered, grabbing the blankets and umbrella.

With some struggling, we finally reached sand.

Now, I usually like to go near the water to set up headquarters, but apparently she had a different agenda. We stood about 50 yards back from the water for about five minutes until she scoped out the area and decided where we would set up camp.

Let me give you a little description of beach culture. I think a sociology student could do a thesis based on the normal ebb and flow of segregation on any given beach. From where we were standing, the lifeguard's chair was off to the right 35 yards or so in front of us at about the one o'clock position. A flock of beautiful, flat-tummied, hard-bodied, tan, young women was gathered around it. I suppose there were guys there too, but who noticed?

Off to the left about the ten o'clock position was the bathroom facility, where the overweight moms of the overactive children usually like to congregate.

Guess where my honey decided to go pitch her umbrella?

After I made a couple of trips back to our parking spot, she set up her little area, sans make-up case, as I had left it in the car because my back couldn't take it. I received surprisingly little argument for its absence, by the way.

She looked great in her swimsuit. I mean, just great. I was very pleasantly surprised. I looked around at our little surfside community and smiled at the knowledge that my girl was the best-looking girl there. Then it hit me. There was a method to her madness. You want to look thin and beautiful? Hang out with the fat and ugly.

"Can you put some lotion on me?" she asked as she flipped on to her stomach.

"Sure. Do you want the sunscreen or the tanning lotion?"

"The lotion. The sunscreen is for you."

"For me?" I laughed. "Baby, in case you haven't noticed, I'm a guy. Guys don't use sunscreen."

"You will fry out here. I am just looking out for you."

"Thanks, babe, but I don't need it," I said while I proceeded to apply the lotion to her back and legs.

I rubbed her in silence for a few minutes. Then a guy emerged from the bathroom and slowly waddled by us. He was older, overweight and balding, and headed right to the porcine family on the next towel. He stopped, turned to me and said, "You'd better put on some sunscreen."

"Thanks, but I don't need it. I'll be fine. Thanks for your concern." I nodded and smiled and then went back to rubbing lotion into my girl's skin.

He came over to me and, with some difficulty, sat on my blanket. "I haven't seen you around here before. I'm Gus. Over there is my family," he tilted his head toward them.

"Nice to meet you, Gus. I'm Larry." I wiped my right hand on the blanket and extended it to him. "I have been coming here for years. I usually sit over there," I said pointing to the lifeguard's chair.

"Ah, yes. I used to be young just like you," he said, with the hint of an accent which I couldn't quite place. "I used to come to the beach by motorcycle with my friends. We used to hang out by the lifeguard's chair, too, and stare at the girls all day long. We'd wear sunglasses so the girls couldn't see us looking." He chuckled, shaking his head.

"Then one day, I met a woman. She wasn't the most beautiful girl in the world, but she was to me. Then we got married, had a few children, and now we come to the beach and sit by the bathroom. Sunbathing with other families like ours is nice. The children all play together and the wives gossip. It's like we have our own little community. It's always nice to welcome someone new here."

"Well, thanks, Gus. That's mighty neighborly of you."

As if he didn't hear me, Gus went on, "I had a beautiful Harley-Davidson motorcycle. The biggest one they made that year. It had a trunk and wind-shield."

He let out a big sigh. "I really miss riding motorcycles. I haven't done that in years. My wife made me sell it to get a minivan so we could take the children and all her stuff to the beach, or to the park, or to her mother's house…" he trailed off looking toward the lifeguard's chair.

Then, as if he just snapped out of a trance, said, "You know, you really are going to burn. You need to put on sunscreen. I never had to use it before, but now I do." He chuckled again and said, "Age, I guess."

He rolled over on his back, flailed his arms and legs trying to get up, and for a brief second, Kafka's vermin from *The Metamorphosis* was there before me.

Later that night, I began to reflect on that chance encounter with Gus. I thought about our conversation and started analyzing in depth, the great migration from the lifeguard's chair to the fat farm by the bathroom. Was it all some sort of crazy metaphor? Was it really analogous to our own existence? After all, I had all the time in the world to think about all of this. I was laid up in bed with the worst sunburn I have ever had in my life.

Ψ

Lesson Learned

When it comes to skincare, listen to your woman. If you don't, you will probably wind up in bed with a terrible sunburn, praying for a big Gus of wind.

LOOKinG FOr Mr. GOODmeal

I walked into my apartment after a long hard day, took off my shoes, grabbed a soda from the fridge and listened to the three messages on my answering machine. Two were from solicitors, but the third was from my girlfriend.

"Hi, baby. I got off work early and I went to the store to get groceries. Then I thought, 'I know he eats out all the time and he probably hasn't had a home cooked meal in a while, so why don't I just come over to his place and cook us some dinner?' Surprise, honey. I will be there about 5:30. You don't have to do anything but sit there and look cute." She made the kissy noise and then I heard the beep.

I thought that was so thoughtful, she was going to make me dinner. I looked at my watch. Holy Moly! She'd be here in ten minutes.

I looked around. What a mess this place was. I'd better clean up and fast. I didn't need her thinking I was a total slob.

Before I knew it, the doorbell rang. I put the last of my things away and answered the door.

"Hi, sweetie," she said. "Could you help me bring up the rest of the bags?" She handed me the bag she had.

"Sure, no problem," I put the bag in the kitchen and went downstairs.

I must've been taking a while because she came downstairs after me and appeared worried. That was until she saw me struggling trying to close her car door while holding six bags of groceries and a flimsy cardboard case of Diet Pepsi.

"Why do you have to take everything at once?" she queried. "Just make two trips."

Apparently, she didn't understand the stronger sex. I just shook my head and laughed. "Hon, men *never* make two trips when they can get everything in one. It's a rule. Uh, could you lock the door, please?"

She shut and locked the door. "Why make it difficult? Let me take a couple of bags."

"No, no, no. I got it. Thanks, though."

"Are you sure?"

"Yup. I got it. Go on back inside and I'll be there in a minute."

Ha, ha, ha! Virility wins!

She looked back at me and shook her head as she walked up the path to the apartment.

The walkway was on an incline, flanked by two hills of lawn on either side. From where the car was to the front door of the building, it was quicker to scale the grassy mound than to walk down the sidewalk to the walkway. Quicker, yes, but much more treacherous.

My girlfriend re-emerged from the doorway just in time to witness my chasing 12 cans of soda and a head of lettuce down the street.

A little while later we were in my apartment washing the soda cans and I said, "It sure is a good thing that they wrap lettuce in plastic, huh?"

She looked at me, "I don't care if it's wrapped in armor. I'm not going to eat lettuce that you had to peel off the tire of an SUV. We just won't have salad tonight."

"Aw, baby, I'm sorry. I'll make it up to you. I'll go to the store to get another head of lettuce."

"No, sweetie, we're already here. We just will forego the salad. There are plenty of other things to eat. We're having veal and steamed vegetables. You go sit down and relax." She pushed me out of the kitchen.

"Ok, but my offer still stands if you find out you cannot possibly live without a salad," I smiled.

I thought: Wasn't she just a doll? Making me dinner.

I sat on the couch and turned on the tube.

"Honey," she called. "What's this?"

"What's what?"

She walked into the living room holding one of my tools.

"Oh, uh, it's a hammer." I smiled.

"I know that. Could you tell me why it was in the cabinet on top of the dishes?"

"Uh, I was using it to hang the clock in the kitchen."

"So, why is it in the cabinet?" she asked again.

"I had to put it somewhere quickly."

"So, you put it in the kitchen cabinet on top of the dishes."

"Uh, yup."

She handed me the hammer and walked back into the kitchen shaking her head.

I heard some rustling and banging in the kitchen drawers and she came back into the living room a few minutes later.

"Baby, where's your bread knife and cutting board?"

"Bread knife?"

"Do you even own a bread knife?"

I was perplexed. "What's a bread knife?"

"Ok, it doesn't have to be a bread knife. Do you have a big knife?"

"Oh, sure. I'll get it." I got up from the couch, went to the hall closet and opened my toolbox. "Here ya go," I said as I handed her a long serrated knife.

"Why is this knife in your toolbox?" she asked.

"Well, I was outside putting in a back-up alarm in my truck—you know, the one that goes beep, beep, beep, beep, when you put the car in reverse…"

"Yeah, I get it. What does that have to do with the knife?"

"I needed something sharp to strip the wires."

"So, you used a kitchen knife?"

"Yeah. Resourceful, ain't I?"

"Tell me," she asked. "Are there any other things I should know about?"

I thought for a second. "No. No, I don't think so. No."

"Ok, then." She stopped and tilted her head up. "What's that smell?"

"What smell?"

"Oh my God, something is burning."

"I don't smell anything," I said as she ran back into the kitchen.

The house was starting to get really smoky. It was coming from the kitchen, or rather from the oven, specifically.

She opened the oven door and a large cloud of smoke wafted up. She waved it away, but not before the smoke detector went off.

She turned off the oven that she had turned on to make the garlic bread for which she needed the knife, and then grabbed the broom that was wedged between the fridge and wall to wave away the smoke from the detector.

When all the smoke cleared she looked in the oven.

"What's this?" she asked holding up a smoldering cloth.

"Uh, I don't know."

"Don't give me that. You know, you just won't admit it."

"Ok, ok. It's what's left of my underwear."

"And what," she pointed to the burnt cloth, "is your underwear doing in the oven?"

"Well, you might as well know. You were coming over and I didn't have time to clean up the house, so I just put stuff away just to get it out of sight."

"Don't you have a cleaning woman come in?" she asked. (See the chapter titled *Propinkwity*.)

I nodded slowly. "I had to let her go. She was stealing."

"Well, then, why didn't you put the underwear in the hamper?"

"For two reasons. One, it was too far away, and time was of the essence—it was literally seconds before you arrived—and two, it was full of magazines."

"Why is your hamper full of magazines?"

"I had to get them off the bathroom floor because I knew you would be coming over."

"Ok, now you are really starting to worry me. You read dirty magazines in the bathroom?"

"No, no, no. Nothing like that. They're car magazines. As a matter of fact, the last one was the one that told me how to wire the back-up alarm in the truck that I needed the big knife for."

She looked around the apartment and laughed. Then she said, "You cleaned up in a hurry because I was coming over and you didn't want me to see your dirty apartment? That is just so cute." She put her arms around me and kissed me.

Then she added, "You know you're taking me out to dinner, right?"

Ψ

Lesson Learned

No matter how cute and quirky your habits may seem at the beginning of your relationship, later on, however, this quirkiness will grate on her nerves so badly that she may want to hit you on the head with a hammer. That is, if she can find it. [HINT: Try hiding it under the wire stripper.]

Onesies, Twosies, Menses, Bluesies

When you're in love everything is just so wonderful. The sky is wonderful, the trees are wonderful, the rain is wonderful, the bills are wonderful, traffic is wonderful, long lines are wonderful, having your teeth drilled without Novocain is wonderful. *Everything* is just so wonderful.

Wonderful, indeed, except that first dreaded encounter that brings you off of cloud nine. It is the very thing that makes men quake with fear, the thing that no man could ever hope to comprehend. It is the most volatile of all mood swings—PMS.

Every woman experiences this at one time or another, but most of them tell you they never get it. It's always the other girls that get it.

My first experience with my girlfriend's pre-menstrual syndrome occurred on our first road trip together, about three weeks after we started dating exclusively.

I have never been to Canada but I've always wanted to go, so my girlfriend and I decided to take a long weekend and do just that. I drove.

I am big on documenting trips with my camera, so when we arrived at the border, I held up the camera to the border guard.

"Put that camera down, now!" he yelled.

My girlfriend slapped me in the arm.

I looked at the guard then at my girlfriend, and put the camera on the seat. I felt like a toddler that found his mother's vibrator. I don't know what I was more shocked over—the guard yelling at me, or my girlfriend hitting my arm.

"What is the nature of your visit?" the guard asked.

I leaned out the window.

"Purely pleasure," I winked as I answered. He didn't laugh.

"Do you have any alcohol, tobacco or weapons on your person or in your vehicle?" he asked.

"Uh, no, not that I know of."

"Do you have cash on your person or in your vehicle in excess of $10,000?" he asked.

I turned to my girlfriend and started laughing. "He said, 'Do you have cash on your person in excess of $10,000?'"

My girlfriend wasn't laughing. So I turned back to the guard. He wasn't laughing either.

"Sir, can I ask you to pull your car around to the first stall over there and wait for an officer?" he said as he pointed.

"Now, you did it," my girlfriend said. "This isn't a place where you should make jokes."

"Sheesh, I'm sorry. I didn't know they'd be so anal." I drove to the stall to which the officer pointed.

After sitting there for a half hour watching a customs agent give my truck a full-body cavity search, we were on our way.

"Do you have to make jokes all the time?" she asked. "I'm so embarrassed. That guy went through my bag. I have personal things in there." She seemed really annoyed.

"I'm sorry, ok? How many times do I have to apologize? I thought you loved my sense of humor."

"Just not today, ok?" She then proceeded to take out a mirror and fuss with her face.

For the rest of our drive to the hotel we sat in silence save for one question she asked me—"Do you have any chocolate?"

We arrived at the hotel and checked in.

This time I was prepared for all of her stuff (see the chapter titled *The Beach Is Back*). I brought a handtruck.

We got the room key and I ferried the luggage to the elevator, up the seven stories, and out to the room. We stood in front of the door.

My girlfriend rolled her eyes and stuck her hand out. "The key?"

I stood the handtruck upright and put down the three bags I had on my shoulders. I reached into my pocket and handed her the card key.

She opened the door and immediately said, "We're not staying in this room. This is a smoking room. We specifically requested a non-smoking room. The stench here is just unbearable. We have to change rooms. This is unacceptable."

She threw her arms up and continued, "Oh, this is so frustrating. I am starving and I have to deal with this."

I agreed with her about the room odor, so I carted the luggage back down the hall, into the elevator, down the seven floors and back to the front desk.

The clerk was very apologetic and obliging and gave us a non-smoking room.

I, again, ferried the luggage to the elevator, up eight stories this time, and out to the room. We stood in front of the door.

My girlfriend rolled her eyes and stuck her hand out. "The key?"

I stood the handtruck upright and put down the three bags I had on my shoulders. I reached into my pocket and handed her the card key.

She opened the door and walked in. I followed with the luggage.

She went over to the window and looked out. "Look, there are balconies in those other rooms. I want a balcony."

"It's probably more money, babe," I said as I prayed I didn't have to get a different room.

"I want a balcony." Then she added, "And I'm hungry."

"Ok, ok."

I carted the luggage back down the hall, into the elevator, down the eight floors and back to the front desk.

The clerk was very accommodating. No extra charge for the room with a balcony. So, I, yet again, ferried the luggage to the elevator, up six stories this time, and out to the room. We stood in front of the door.

My girlfriend rolled her eyes and stuck her hand out.

"I know, I know. The key." I said.

I stood the handtruck upright and put down the three bags I had on my shoulders. I reached into my pocket and handed her the card key.

She opened the door and walked in. I followed with the luggage.

This was more like it. The room was to her liking and I was done carting the luggage around.

She grabbed something out of one of her bags and went to the bathroom.

After she was done, she came back out.

"I need to eat. I am positively famished," she said.

"Ok, just let me go to the bathroom. It's my turn."

"Can't you go downstairs?" she asked.

"You didn't go downstairs. You went here. I want to go here, too."

She folded her arms. Then she said, "Will you hurry up?"

"Baby, I know you're hungry, so why don't you go to the restaurant down-stairs, get a table and order something. Just get me a cheeseburger and I'll be down in a minute, ok?"

"Ok, fine." With that, she walked out and closed the door behind her.

I let out a sigh. I asked myself: *Boy was she being a total bitch or what? What men put up with—it just boggles the mind.*

I went to the bathroom. In there I saw something I have never seen before.

Next to the toilet was, uh, another toilet. One with a spigot and a drain. It looked like a birdbath for midgets. Then I realized that this must be a bidet. I have never seen one before, but it dawned on me that we were in a foreign country with a European influence. Of course there would be a bidet.

I was so intrigued. I just had to try it.

After some twisting of knobs and figuring out the logistics (it didn't have a manual for us dumb Americans), I assumed the position, as it were, and strad-dled the porcelain contraption.

I really thought I did everything correctly, except one minor thing, which I figured out later—I was sitting on it backwards.

The water was shooting up with such pressure that my nuts were jammed up into my throat. Needless to say this didn't feel good in the least.

I tried to reach behind me to turn it off but I couldn't do it without water shooting up my ass with the velocity of a scud. They should use this thing for riot control.

I did all I could to try to shut the water without getting up, but I couldn't. I had to just bite the bullet and get off.

The second I got off, water shot up the back of my shirt like a freaking whip. I tried to jump out of the way, but it was hard to do with my pants around my ankles, so I fell into the bathtub.

Meanwhile, the geyser is spraying water all over the bathroom floor. I climbed out of the tub and scurried over to the bidet (my soaking wet pants were still around my soaking wet ankles) to turn off the water.

Just as the water stopped there was a knock at the front door.

Mustering up the utmost nonchalance, I said, "Who is it?"

"It's me. I didn't take the card key and I need to get something from the bathroom," said my girlfriend.

Relieved that it was my girlfriend and not the fire department, I put a towel around my waist, and opened the door.

She pushed past me and went right into the bathroom where she stopped dead in her tracks. She looked at the flood and then looked at me.

I stood before her with my pants around my ankles, a towel around my middle, dripping wet from head to toe.

"What happened here?" she asked.

"Uh, nothing. Just a little accident," I said as I tried to smile.

"I can see that," she said. "Well, I had a little accident myself. I just got my period, so if you'll excuse me, I need to use the bathroom."

She closed the door.

It was ok with me that she got her period. We wouldn't have had sex anyway until I shit my testicles back out.

Then she said through the door, "Call room service. Have them bring up some towels, a pot of coffee, a pint of black raspberry ice cream, and a bottle of Motrin."

Make that *two* bottles of Motrin.

Ψ

Lesson Learned

If you want your relationship to work out with your woman you must do the things on this list:

1. Keep a bottle of Motrin around at all times.

2. Keep a chocolate bar within easy reach.

3. Memorize Dr. Jekyll's cycle dates so you could avoid being in a confined space for an entire weekend with Ms. Hyde.

4. Take a course on European plumbing.

The Winds of Change

I didn't know what the hell she put in those meatballs, but I had so much gas OPEC sent me a membership form.

It was my birthday. Normally for my birthday I'd like to go to a restaurant and then do an insipid activity, like bowling, or pool, or something like that. I don't usually like to make a big deal out of it, but since my girlfriend and I were only going together for a few months and this would be my first birthday spent with her, I left the plans in her hands.

She decided to make me a birthday dinner at her apartment.

Her apartment was small. It was just a studio—maybe six hundred square feet. The couch converted into a bed on the far side of the room, the closet was next to the little kitchenette off in the corner, and the bathroom was next to the refrigerator. The dining table was next to a small fish tank, which split the room in two, giving the kitchen separation from the living quarters.

"What's your favorite cuisine?" she asked the day before.

"Oh, baby, don't knock yourself out. Just make me anything Italian and I'll be happy."

So that's what she did. And, I might add, it was fantastic.

First she served us minestrone soup made from scratch, and then an antipasto consisting of romaine lettuce, Genoa and Sicilian salami, fresh mozzarella, some roasted red peppers and vine ripened plum tomatoes.

Then she brought out a heaping plate of good, old-fashioned meatballs and linguine, topped with freshly grated Locatelli Pecorino Romano cheese, and a dollop of ricotta.

We ended the meal with store-bought sfogliatelle and a couple of espressos. It was just out of this world.

"Honey, this was the best birthday dinner I have ever had. It was absolutely delicious. You know, you need to open your own restaurant."

"Oh, stop it, honey. I was glad to do it. It's your birthday and you deserve it." She leaned in and kissed me.

She started removing the dishes from the table. "Now you go relax on the couch while I clean up in here."

I got really comfortable on the couch and closed my eyes. I just sat there enjoying the after-feast glow thinking about how much I really enjoyed that dinner, and how lucky I was to have her in my life.

After about twenty minutes, I felt a sharp stabbing pain in my stomach. It was sharp enough that I bolted upright.

I looked down at my abdomen. I could almost see it swell right before my eyes. If I didn't know any better I'd swear I had had a distended liver.

With each passing second it was getting worse. I did all I could to clench and pucker. It was obviously gas pains from all the spices she put in the meatballs and sauce, but I couldn't go to the bathroom because she would hear it, since it was right next to the kitchen. And I couldn't just let it rip. She already thought I was an utter slob from that underwear burning fiasco at my place (see the chapter titled *Looking For Mr. Goodmeal*); I couldn't let her think I was totally classless. I would be so embarrassed. We haven't crossed that farting-in-front-of-each-other-line yet.

I was squirming on the couch. Beads of sweat formed on my forehead. My stomach was undulating in ten second waves. I didn't know what to do.

Just then the doorbell rang. Perfect! I would get up to answer the door and then somehow get outside to let out my gas.

But, I was too slow. My girlfriend was at the door before I even got off the couch.

"Hi, Laura. Hi, Robert," she said as she opened the door. "What brings you two here?"

Laura was a coworker and friend of my girlfriend, and Robert was her husband. I had met them a number of times these last few months.

"Well, we know it's Larry's birthday and we just wanted to stop off and wish him a happy birthday," said Laura as she stepped into the room. "We brought him a little something."

I'd hoped to all that was holy that she brought some Imodium. No such luck.

"Hi Larry. Happy Birthday," Laura said as she walked toward me with a shiny bag.

I tried to sound as natural as possible.

"Thank you," I said as I took the bag. I put it on the couch and tried to stand up without, uh, breaking the seal, as it were.

My girlfriend closed the door, walked back to the kitchen area and said, "You are just in time for birthday cake. Take off your jackets."

Great. Now I had three people in the apartment I couldn't fart in front of. I possibly could have gotten away with it with just my girlfriend, but now I was stuck. And my stomach was hurting so badly by that point that I thought about eating the charcoal from the water filter in the fish tank. I needed to do something, and I needed to do it fast.

I blurted out, "Thanks, babe. I gotta go." Then I ran to the door and raced out of the apartment. I would deal with the consequences of leaving like that, later.

I ran as fast as I could with a clenched butt, and looked for a dark, secluded place with no one around.

I nestled up against some shrubs, looked left and right, and then let loose. It was loud. It was long. And it was powerful. It was so powerful that I thought I expelled my spine. Afterwards, I let out the biggest sigh I ever had—like some sort of tremendous weight had been lifted off of my shoulders.

I didn't see the old guy standing behind me walking his dog until I turned around. I was mortified.

With my face a bright red I said, "Uh, excuse me."

He looked me up and down, and then he nodded knowingly.

"What?" I asked.

"You're on a blind date fart hold, ain'tcha?"

"Well, not exactly, but you're close," I said, not wishing to elaborate.

"That'll kill you. It's best you just let loose. Hey, we're all human."

He picked his nose as he walked away.

I stood there a minute and thought about it. You know, he was right. So, I propelled myself with my bio-methane back to my girlfriend's apartment to explain.

When I arrived, Laura and Robert were on the couch staring into space, and my girlfriend was in the bathroom. It sounded like Chinese New Year in there.

She's going to be so embarrassed.

Ψ

Lesson Learned

It's never easy to show the disgusting side of yourself to someone who you want to like you. So, contrary to the old man's advice, hold out as long as you can. Let her go first. Then you have carte blanche to do all the Dutch Ovens* you want.

---

* **Dutch Oven:** Farting in bed and holding your partner's head under the covers. Lots of laughs.

Tortured Soles

I should never have said *yes*. That was my first mistake because some things should not ever be witnessed by the male gender.

The question from my girlfriend that prompted my answer of *yes* was every heterosexual, working man's nightmare—"Do you want to come shopping with me?"

I couldn't very well have turned her down. I mean, just last week she sucked it up and came with me to a minor league baseball spring training event so, turn-about is fair play; it was my duty as a boyfriend to accompany her on one of her weekly buying trips to the mall.

She had a whole routine for going shopping depending on the time of year. Let's see. It was the third Saturday of the first month of the change of seasons toward the end of the millennium…so, that meant that we shop for shoes.

I never realized what a dilemma it was for all of you women actually needing so many pairs of shoes to go with your various clothes, moods and, ahem, cycles.

I mean, you need black shoes, brown shoes, red, shoes, blue shoes; tall shoes, short shoes, soft shoes, hard shoes; rubber soles, gum soles, plastic soles, marshmallow soles, leather soles, leather uppers, leather sides, leather insoles; breathable vinyl, breathable cloth, breathable synthetics; short heels, tall heels; with stitching, with piping, with buckles, with buckles, stitching *and* piping, with piping, stitching *and* buckles (this is *not* the same but don't ask me why)—Oh, my God, the list is endless!

We were in every man's favorite place—the mall—and we walked past my favorite discount one-style-fits-all shoe store (their slogan is: *Buy one shoe, get the other one free!*). I pointed to it with sadness, like a toddler with a finger up his nose being dragged by his mother past the cotton candy display at the amusement park.

"Honey, why can't we look in there?" I asked with the utmost sincerity.

"Oh, you are just so cute, sometimes," she said as she shook her head, smiled and forged ahead to the *Mega Expensive Shoes For Diva Wannabees* store.

Once inside, I saw tons of women with hair of all shapes and sizes groping this particular merchandise island of shoes. Shoes were flying everywhere. There was a sea of hands probing, pulling and grasping anything with, or without a sole. There was a huge 70 per cent off sale and, apparently, that's when women shed any form of dignity and self-worth.

It was now time for the 2 o'clock free-for-all at the clearance rack.

I was at once appalled and riveted just watching this whole event unfold before me. I didn't want to watch, but I couldn't turn away.

My girlfriend circled around the unsuspecting shoe-feeders like a puma after a flock of sheep. She searched the rack. She spotted what she wanted. With eyes locked upon the delicious, distressed, burgundy leather sling-backs, she inched slowly toward the pack of wildebeests.

She waited for just the right moment to pounce. There, between the rotund, middle-aged woman with the wattle-like upper arms and the twenty-something bleached-blonde with the push-up bra so tight that her chin now had nipples, was an opening just big enough for my girlfriend to swoop in with her pink claws and snatch the innocent footwear from her unprepared enemies.

My girlfriend leapt at the shoe, but the blonde's reflexes were better than my girlfriend anticipated. Blondie grabbed the left one while my girlfriend grabbed the right one. Both of them were tugging at their respective shoe trying to get the other to let go or, at the very least, snap the plastic tie that held the shoes together.

The variable in this tête-à-tête was the fat woman with the flapping triceps. Whether it was innocent or not, she gave my girlfriend a bump with her rear end that was so violent, I thought it might've caused a perigeal shift. My girlfriend fell upon Blondie who, in turn, fell upon the woman next to her, and so on, like a bunch of human bowling pins.

When the dust settled, my girlfriend wound up, not only with a thigh bruise the size of a soda can, but also with the pair of burgundy sling-backs and a pair of cheap-looking plastic flip-flops that had a UFO disk-like doodad hovering over the big toe. This monstrosity of a shoe, which I knew she would never wear, plus those coveted sling-backs, left her purse $190 lighter. And that's *with* the 70 per cent off. This couldn't possibly have been worth it. But, hey, that's just my opinion.

My second mistake was made that evening when I found three pair of identical distressed, burgundy leather sling-backs, and one pair of UFO-topped flip-flops in her closet and I called her on it.

"Babe," I said holding up an old pair from her closet. "Why did you spend all that money for shoes that you already have? Look, your closet is full of the same stuff you just bought."

"They are not the same," she answered as she showed me a random two side by side. "See here? The toe on this is squarer than the toe on this. And the strap is a different width."

"Oh, yeah. I see that," I lied.

"You are just saying that."

"No, I really see the difference. What I don't see is why you paid so much money for these things to begin with. I mean, it's just a pair of shoes."

"Just because your entire shoe wardrobe consists of a five year old pair of what-used-to-be-white Adidas with no tread on the sole and a pair of brown earth shoes from 1975 which, I hope to God, you never, ever wear in public with me, doesn't mean *I* don't want to have a sense of style."

"You're saying I have no style? Me? Ha! That's a laugh!"

"Honey, let's face it," she said as she put her arm around me. "You're 35 years old and you wear a New York Mets watch."

"Don't be dissing my watch, woman. This is a bona-fide Tom Seaver collectible," I said as I tapped the watch.

"Besides this isn't about me," I added. "It's about you and why you pay so much money for things you already own."

"Honey," she sighed, "it isn't about the shoes itself. It's about the experience getting them. You know the old saying: It's not the destination, it's the journey."

"Judging from your closet you've been taking the same journey for years. I think it's time you find a less dangerous and more inexpensive path."

She stood in thought for a moment. Then she said, "You know, you're right. Next week we'll hit the outlet malls."

Oh, boy. I can hardly wait.

Ψ

Lesson Learned

When you sit in your easy chair and click on the Wrestling Channel or the Wild Predators Network, and your woman starts in on you saying how these types of shows are too violent, reflect upon how women act on sale days at the shoe store. But never, ever, say anything to her because she might mistake the television remote for a pair of burgundy leather sling-backs and dropkick your ass to get it.

Parental Control Advised

"You sure I look alright?" I asked, tugging at my collar.

"You look fine. There's nothing to be nervous about. They'll like you," she assured me.

We were standing on the porch, just about to ring the bell to her parents' house. This was the first time I was going to meet them and, I don't mind telling you, I was dreading every minute. She had already briefed me on her dad's drinking.

She pushed the doorbell and a few seconds later the door opened.

The only thing I saw were arms coming out of the doorway. Then I heard a cry which sounded somewhere between a stepped-on cat and a freight train whistle. This of course was her mother hugging her daughter like this was the first time she'd seen her since she put her up for adoption 30 years ago. Truth was they had spent the day together shopping.

The door opened wider and a man's hand came out. "You must be Larry." The alcohol on his breath could have lit all the lamps in Jerusalem. It wasn't even five o'clock and he was toasted.

"Yes, sir. Very nice to meet you."

"Don't call me sir. That was my father," he smirked and kind of rocked his head from side to side with some sort of pride as if he were the one to make up that phrase. I could tell it was going to be a long night.

"Come in, dear, sit down," invited her mother as she hugged me.

We entered the house, which was furnished in, what I like to think of as, '70s gauche. The whole house seemed to be awash in avocado green, save for the burnt orange shag carpeting in the living room. There was a lot of chrome and glass around the house, as well a few dusty pictures of Ronald Reagan.

Her father asked, "Anyone care for a scotch?"

Uh, no thanks. The last thing I want to do was to get drunk with you here in Brady Bunch hell while you interrogate me for all my deepest, darkest secrets, and whether or not I had sex with your daughter. Not in your wildest dreams would I even consider it. No effin' way.

"Sure, I'd love one." I said out of politeness. I figured I would just nurse it all night.

"Dinner will be in about thirty minutes," her mom said. "So, you boys just get yourselves acquainted. Sit down, Larry, make yourself comfortable."

I knew it. It was a conspiracy. First the scotch, then the late dinner. They're going to drug me, take me to the mother ship, and probe every orifice I have. They'll study me like some sort of lab rat and then set me free with no recollection of the event until I'm driving down a deserted road in Kansas thirty years from now and recognize some scorch marks in a wheat field.

"Yes," I answered back, "It'll be fun."

"So, Larry. I'm told you are a truck driver. Do you drive over the road?"

No, I drive all over people's lawns. Chews 'em up real good.

"No, sir, not that kind of truck driver," I answered, knowing he meant cross-country long haul driving. "Mostly around the city here."

"What kind of things do you haul?"

I would like to haul my ass out of here. Preferably to another state. But that would make me an over-the-road trucker, and I wouldn't want to lie to you, seeing how you had a big part in manufacturing my girlfriend and all.

"Mostly restaurant paper products. You know, cups, plates, to-go containers, bags, foils—things like that."

"Oh, so you visit lots of restaurants then, huh?"

You sure are as sharp as a tack.

"Yes, as a matter of fact, I met your daughter in one of my favorite restaurants on my route."

"Yes, she told me," he said as he swallowed another sip of scotch.

So, if you know, then what the hell are you asking me for? I feel like a defendant at the McCarthy hearings.

"You a Republican or a Democrat?" he asked without any rhyme or reason.

Great, just what I need. Political chitchat with Foster Brooks.

Before I could muster up an answer, he blurted out another non sequitur. "You're Catholic, aren't you?"

I had to try to find a tactful way to avoid his questions. There were a few minutes of uncomfortable silence, and to break it, I stood up and walked over to a dusty glass shelf full of old photographs. He came sauntering over.

"This here was our little girl when she was five. She was cute as a button. Over here is a picture of her with her sister and brother back in '81. I remember that because that's when Reagan got shot." His voice trailed off, and he looked into space.

Oh, boy.

I immediately grabbed another photo. It was a picture of a young blonde girl about twenty years old or so, yet was dated 1965.

"Who is this? She is really cute." I asked.

"That there is a picture of my wife when I met her. She sure was beautiful."

"You're kidding?" I was pleasantly surprised. "Wow. She looked a little like Peggy Lee."

"That she did." He took the last sip of his drink and murmured, "Now she looks like General Lee."

He looked at his glass. "Hey, do you want another drink? I think I'll have one."

"Yeah, you know what? I think I will have another." I then proceeded to gulp my drink down.

Twenty minutes later, the girls came in telling us dinner is ready. There we were with my arm around him and his face buried in my shoulder. He was sobbing.

"What's going on here?" asked my girlfriend, incredulously.

"I don't know, babe. We had a couple of drinks and started talking politics. When I told him Spiro Agnew resigned his vice-presidency on my twelfth birthday, he broke down."

Ψ

Lesson Learned

When you meet her parents for the first time, it's a good idea to do some research on the things they feel passionate about. Then you have some ammunition if they back you in a corner. Plus if the tactic of getting your girlfriend to like you by getting her drunk and making her cry the night of your first date worked on her, then you should yield the same results from the parents. After all, the apple doesn't fall far from the tree.

The FlyinG NOne

"Larry, this is my sister and her husband," my girlfriend said with a wave of her hand.

"Pleased to meet you," I nodded, but I really wasn't. I just said that.

I was actually a little disappointed because it was our first weekend together in a long time due to work and other commitments, and I just wanted to spend it alone with her. Unbeknownst to me, she had other plans that involved her sister and brother-in-law spending Saturday night at her place because they would be away on vacation for two weeks starting Monday. Yes, I knew I had to meet them sometime, but I just didn't want it to be this weekend.

My girlfriend and her sister are very close. She had said on a previous date with me that they tell each other everything. *Everything.*

I'm always apprehensive of getting into a relationship with a woman who tells her sister everything. I wondered if her sister really did know everything, like what my favorite dessert is or just how good I am in bed. Or, for that matter, how bad.

Did they stay up nights talking to each other on the phone laughing at the expense of my genitalia? Did they question whether my boobs were just as big as theirs? Did they elbow each other when a beefy, hunky guy came on TV? Did they question each other's taste in men, saying that age-old statement, "You could do better than him?" Did they paint each other's nails pink? I'd bet the farm they did. I also had a sneaking suspicion that the rules of confidentiality did not apply. I'd bet the ol' brother-in-law knew certain select tidbits, too.

My girlfriend escorted us all into the living room section of her studio apartment, where there were drinks and a small platter of hors d'oeuvres waiting to be ingested. My girlfriend's brother-in-law made a beeline for the booze.

Tall, lanky, and with eyes that seemed a bit too sunken, he seemed to be a quiet, unassuming guy. Yeah, a quiet unassuming guy who downed two gin and tonics in five minutes. Well, they do say a girl winds up marrying her father, you know.

Time ticked away, but the conversation never really came around to the men. The women monopolized it in a hurry. I got the feeling that Brother-In-Law here had been through this a lot due to his blank gaze.

"Excuse me, how long have you two been married?" I asked Brother-In-Law.

His wife stopped babbling about some sale somewhere long enough to interject.

"Next year will be eight years although we've been together ten," she said. Then she went back to talking to my girlfriend.

I turned my head from her to him. "Wow, together ten years, huh? Do you have any kids?"

Again, his wife stopped talking to my girlfriend long enough to blurt out, "We have three." And, again, she resumed her conversation.

Couldn't the freaking guy answer for himself?

I couldn't resist: "One of each, huh?"

All three of them looked at me like I just brought a golf club to batting practice.

"We have two boys and a girl. Six, five and two," she explained.

"Oh. I see." Then I asked her husband, "So, are you taking the kids with you on vacation?"

She jumped in quickly. "Oh, no, we are just going ourselves. Mom is watching the children."

I tried very hard not to be disingenuous. "Oh, how great for you guys."

I didn't even bother looking at Brother-In-Law anymore. I figured she would never let her lesser half speak. It had probably been this way for—let me guess—ten years or so?

"Where are you going?" I asked.

She straightened herself up on the couch. With a certain pride in her manner, she looked directly at me. "You are going to be so jealous when I tell you."

I admit now I was a tad curious. I expected her to say someplace romantic like Paris, or Monaco, or perhaps Rio, or Rome.

"Where?" I asked with great anticipation.

"Banff."

"Banff?"

"Yes. Banff."

"The Banff in Canada?"

"The very one," she nodded.

I tried not to look her in the eye. "No kidding. Wow, I *am* jealous."

"My husband travels so much on his job that all of his frequent flyer miles paid for the airfare," she added.

"That's great." I said.

Ok, I'd had enough. Looking for a quick way out of there, I thought I would use the out-of-alcohol angle.

"Oh, my. I see we are out of gin. I don't have a problem going to the store for more," I offered as I got up to get my jacket.

Banff's Minister of Tourism turned to her husband, "Honey, why don't you go with him? It'll give us girls a chance to chat."

A chance to chat? What the hell have you girls been doing, pre-chat warm-ups?

I really didn't want to take Drunken Lurch with me to the store, but I thought this would be a good time for me to have a chat of my own. I kissed my girlfriend and then we left.

Once in the car, I started the conversation. "So, I bet you really love these little get-togethers, huh?

After a long pause he said, "Yeah."

"Well, I'm finally glad I've gotten a chance to meet you guys. I've heard a lot about you."

Another long pause. "Yeah."

I thought: Well, I see we are quite loquacious now, aren't we? I figured I'd try another approach.

"I, uh, don't mean to pry," I started, "but, I hear you, uh, have a little problem. Do you want to talk about it? Man to man, I mean."

I was fishing. Grasping at straws. Probing for some sort of insight into their family and what I am getting myself into.

His eyes got really wide. He looked like he was going to hyperventilate.

"She told you?" he asked while he rubbed is palms on his lap.

Aha! Now, we're getting somewhere. See, I told you—everything. They tell each other everything.

"Relax," I said. "It's ok. It's happened to me, too." I still needed more information, so I tried to be as comforting as possible.

He looked at me with those sunken blood-shot puppy-dog eyes. "Really?"

"Yup, really. You can talk to me if you want. Our conversation doesn't leave this car, ok?"

He acquiesced. "Well, it seems to be always happening lately. It's gotten to the point where I really don't want to do it any more," he confessed.

"What seems to happen lately?"

"It's really personal."

"I know," I said. "I know. It's ok. Talk to me."

"Well, once I get inside," he started, "my head starts to really hurt and I get nauseated."

"You're kidding? Your, uh, head hurts?" I was riveted.

"Yes. And it doesn't matter if I recline, sit up, or stand. It hurts all ways."

"Wow." Together ten years and they still did it standing up. I was enthralled. Maybe this guy wasn't the loser I thought he was.

"Go on."

"I've tried cold compresses, tugging on my ears, and a blindfold. Sometimes a combination of all three."

Sheesh! This guy was kinky.

Then he added, "The worst part is that when I, uh, arrive, my ears get so clogged. Larry, I tell you, I can't stand it, anymore."

"Holy crap. That's awful."

"It's gotten to the point where I need to be really toasted in order for me to even do it at all. Now, I'm drinking more because of it. Tell me," he turned to me, "how do you handle it?"

"Well, I saw the doctor and he prescribed something called Viagra. But, I'm not experiencing the penile pain and clogged ears that you do."

"Penile pain? Viagra?" He was stupefied. "I don't have penile pain, and I don't need Viagra."

"What do you mean?"

"I'm talking about flying. I get really sick flying."

"Oh."

Well at least my girlfriend didn't tell her sister about my, uh, inability to fly. *But, I'm sure Charles Lindbergh here will.*

Ψ

Lesson Learned

You should always be a little bit wary of your woman's sororal relationships, but not to the point you obsess over it. Otherwise you will get mad and say something you will regret. Then you will have one of those sore-oral relationships yourself.

Santa Clawed

It is my belief that you can kind of judge a person by the type of animal they like. Some people like horses, which says to me that they are strong and majestic. Some people like ferrets, which says to me they are quiet folk who may feel the need to stand out from the crowd. Some people like birds, which might suggest someone is a free spirit. Some people like reptiles, which some other people might find repugnant; might imply the person is strong-willed with an air of mysticism. But most people, I think, fall into the dog/cat category. And, although neither one of us had any animals, I am what you would call a dog-person and my girlfriend was a cat-person. She came from a long line of cat-people, beginning with the matriarch of her family, her maternal grandmother.

Now, there are cat-people and there are cat-freaking-crazy-people. The latter would describe her grandmother. I understand having a cat or two, or if the place is big enough, maybe three. But, I'm pretty sure that ten cats would qualify you as a cat-freaking-crazy person. Under this criterion, that would make my girlfriend's grandmother a first-class, grade A, 100 per cent loon. Fifteen cats is just way over the top.

That first year we were dating, we went to her grandmother's house for Christmas. There were some decorative lights around the place, but nothing too awe-inspiring. As we walked up to the front door, I noticed some lumpy shadows across the lawn, which made it look more like Halloween than Christmas. The lumpy shadows appeared to be moving, and it was kind of freaking me out, until my girlfriend said it was just cats.

"Just cats?" I squinted towards the lawn. "Ok. How many does she have? That sure looks like a hell of a lot of lumps."

She mumbled something inaudibly.

"Excuse me? I didn't hear you. How many cats, babe?"

"Fifteen, ok? She has fifteen cats."

"Fifteen cats?" I repeated. "I don't even have fifteen dollars. Doesn't that strike you as a bit odd?"

"No, not particularly. You never have any money."

"Not me, Miss Sarcasm, your grandmother. Don't you think having fifteen cats is a bit, um, neurotic?"

"Ever since Grandpa died she has adopted cats to keep her company. She's lonely. What can I say?"

"Do you realize she has more cats than the United States has Supreme Court Justices?"

"Yes, dear. Let's just try to have a nice Christmas dinner, ok? It's only for a little while," she kissed me and then rang the doorbell.

An old lady opened the door. She was slight in stature and wrinkled as a walnut. "Hello, darling," she said as she cupped my girlfriend's cheek. "Come on inside. Your parents and brother are here."

Just as I walked in the door, the acrid smell of cat urine and mothballs wafted up to my nostrils. I thought I was going to pass out. If they had used this in Viet Nam instead of mustard gas, we would have won.

To the right of the foyer was the living room; to the left was the dining room. I went to the living room to put our coats on the sofa and gifts under the tree. The sofa was torn to shreds from the cats sharpening their claws on it and the tree looked pretty sickly as well. Maybe it was dying from the smell.

Two cats were fighting on the sofa, three or four were climbing on the furniture, and one was swinging like Tarzan from the tree to the windowsill on a vine of garland.

I had to get out of there. "Honey," I yelled, "where's the bathroom?"

"Upstairs, sweetheart."

Upstairs I went. To the bathroom. The bathroom full of cats. Big surprise there.

I swear those cats were like boomerangs. I would put them out of the bathroom; they'd come back in before I could shut the door. It was like a game. A game I was quickly losing.

After a while I had a cat on each arm and one on each pant leg clinging to dear life. I hobbled out of the bathroom like Frankenstein and wildly flailed each appendage so those relentless felines would be flung downstairs. Mission accomplished, I hurried back to the bathroom and slammed the door.

Once inside with the door shut I noticed that the stench was markedly stronger. I walked past the sink to the toilet listening to the little crunchy sounds my feet made with each step. I sure hoped that was kitty litter.

There were a couple of litter boxes on the floor next to the toilet. Both were pretty full. I stood in front of the toilet, held my breath, unzipped my fly, and proceeded to do my business. Just then I was startled by something touching my leg. One of those damn critters stood up on its hind legs, and held out its paw.

With talons exposed, it swatted my leg and proceeded to dig its claw into my thigh. I screamed and jumped. Urine and kitty litter were flying everywhere. The cat hissed. I punched it in the face.

It flew off me and I opened the door and ran down the stairs.

My girlfriend must've heard the commotion because she was at the bottom of the stairs yelling up to me, "Larry, what's wrong?"

"What's wrong? What's wrong? I'll tell you what's wrong! One of these freaking cats attacked me!"

"Oh, honey you're exaggerating," she said in disbelief.

She must have seen the look of horror on my face because then she said, "You're breathing so hard. Calm down and tell me what happened."

"I was minding my own business, when all of a sudden out of nowhere, this freaking puma grabbed hold of my leg like I was a gazelle on Mutual of Omaha's Wild Kingdom. Look! His freaking claw is still in my thigh!" I looked down to show her and became aware that Little Larry was hanging out, just keeping an eye on things. I put him back as fast as I could and zipped up my sopping wet pants hoping nobody noticed. I looked up just in time to see that Grandma and the rest of her family had congregated around me.

Later that night, as we were driving home from the emergency room, she said, "Thank you very much for embarrassing me in front of my family. And on Christmas, of all days."

"It wasn't my fault. I was attacked."

"Honey, you gave my grandmother's cat a fat lip."

"I don't know why everyone is making this out to be such a big deal. I took it to the emergency room, didn't I?"

Ψ

Lesson Learned

If something happens to her things, no matter how small, she will always make a huge deal out of it regardless of your medical condition. If you slip and fall off a ladder as you are hanging her great grandmother's family heirloom chandelier, and one of the little crystals happens to get a crack in it, you will be hearing about it for the rest of the nine-month rehabilitation for your fractured femur. So, here the advice is simple. No matter how many times she knocks you down, you have to make sure to land on your feet.

TiPtoe Through The TWO LiPS

I'm ticklish. There are no two ways about it. Pretty much anywhere on my body is a T-zone—from the back of my neck, to my underarms, from my ribs, to my feet. *Especially* my feet.

This is why, as much as I tried, I couldn't understand how women went to the spa to get a pedicure. I could understand the painting nails thing, but the scrubbing and scraping that goes on with the underside of the feet—I just could not fathom how they put up with that.

One day, I'd gotten an unexpected bonus at work. So, I decided to spend it on my woman; making her happy made me happy.

I took her to her favorite salon/spa and ordered the works. Whatever she wanted, she could have. From soup to nuts. She decided on a frosting (that sounded to me like something that involved milk), a manicure, and a pedicure.

We arrived at the salon and waited about 15 minutes before being called.

I was all set to just sit in the waiting area but the girl offered me the option to go back and sit with my girlfriend while she gets all this done.

"Wow, I feel like I'm going backstage to see the Rockettes."

Both girls chuckled, although it sounded a bit insincere to me.

First thing on the agenda was the hair. My girlfriend disappeared into a closet for a few minutes. She emerged wearing some doctor scrubs and sat down in what looked to me like something from a *Lost in Space* garage sale.

Having been asked to come back to watch the whole process made me feel like I was privy to some sort of cult ritual. I suppose I expected some sort of operating table, a machine with tons of dials, chains, pulleys, and an electrical storm. But, up to that point everything seemed pretty normal. In an odd way, I was slightly disappointed.

I sat in a chair next to my girlfriend while the beautician went to work. From my pocket, I whipped out the Popular Mechanics magazine that I had bought earlier. I was pretty proud of myself that I had the foresight to bring something with which to occupy my time.

I don't know how long I was engrossed in my magazine. I was reading about that year's SEMA show and an article on Must-Have-Definitely-Cannot-Live-Without-Even-If-It-Means-Your-Wife-Will-Kick-Your-Ass-Out-Of-Your-House-Tools-For-Under-$5,000. I set the magazine down and stretched.

That's when I saw her.

I blanched.

And screamed. Actually, it was more like a bleat.

My girlfriend had on a rubber cap and few strands of hair were poking through at various intervals. She looked like that maniacal doll from The Twilight Zone.

All eyes were upon me because of my little outburst. After I apologized and assured them it won't happen again, I decided it was best to leave for a while.

I killed a couple of hours and then came back to the salon. My girlfriend's hair was done and it looked fantastic. She was just finishing up her manicure (yes, that dreaded pink) and they were escorting her to the pedicure area. I decided to go with her to watch.

The pedicure units were lined up six in a row. It looked more like an arcade game than anything else. They were huge comfy massaging chairs attached to a mini bathtub. I assumed the bathtub was where one would put one's feet to soak, although I still had this incredible urge to put in my quarter and play the virtual boat race game.

My girlfriend climbed into the chair with her freshly painted, pink fingertips splayed. I helped her off with her shoes and stood next to her.

The pedicurist adjusted the temperature of the water, put in some chemicals, and set my girlfriend's feet in the tub.

"Hi, my name is Mary. Have you picked out a color?" she asked my girlfriend.

"Baby, can I pick out the color?" I asked my girlfriend.

From her answer I could tell she really didn't want me to.

"No," she said.

"Why not?" I asked.

"Because they have to match my fingernails."

"Why?" I asked.

Her answer cleared up a lot of the questions I had regarding the ambiguity revolving around the philosophy of a woman's ritual of digit painting.

"It just does."

I paused for a second, and then I asked her, "How about red?"

"Honey..." She gave me a glaring look.

"Something in a deep, dark red. Yeah, that's it—a nice merlot color."

"Honey, please stop it."

Mary pulled up a stool, sat in front of my girlfriend's feet and started cuticle cutting.

I turned to Mary. "Do you have anything in a burgundy?"

She looked at my girlfriend for approval.

"We'll go with the pink, thank you." Then to me: "It's going to be pink, and that's all I want to hear about it. Now, could you do me a favor and lessen the massaging action on my chair, please? It's a little rough and I don't want to mess up my nails."

"Sure," I said as I pressed a button on her armrest.

I looked over at the person sitting two chairs away.

It was a guy.

And he was getting his feet done.

I leaned into my girlfriend and whispered, "Are you kidding me? There's a guy over there getting a pedicure."

"Men get pedicures all the time," replied my girlfriend.

"Well, I'm never gonna do it." I sat in the vacant massage-chair-tub-thing next to my girlfriend, pulled out my magazine, and mumbled something about betting anyone in the joint that the guy two chairs over never operated a chain saw.

Mary came over and started the massaging action on the chair in which I was sitting. She smiled and said, "You'll like it. Relax while I finish your wife's feet."

I quickly blurted out, "She's just my girlfriend. We aren't married."

"Well you should be. You look so cute together."

I sat back in the chair, smiled, nodded and buried myself in my magazine.

The pedicurist resumed her position on the stool. I peered over the magazine and saw her planing my girlfriend's foot with a cheese grater. And she was doing it with gusto.

"Doesn't that hurt?" I asked my girlfriend.

"No, baby. It's fine. It takes away the callous skin and makes my feet smooth."

"She looks like she's scraping barnacles off your hull."

"You know what?" she asked in a revelatory tone. "I think you should get a pedicure so you will see just how good it feels."

"I agree," interjected Mary. "I think you should, too. You will feel much better afterwards."

"No way."

"Come on, baby. That guy over there is doing it," said my girlfriend.

"No effin' way." I folded my arms.

"Aw, sweetheart. For me?" She batted her eyes in that coy way that girls do, to manipulate us men into thinking we would be getting some later if we just do what they want now.

All men know the drill. They know they never get some later. Yet we men all have that glimmer of hope that makes us yield to their wishes. "Ok, you win. We'll try it."

I turned to Mary and joked, "Could I have something in a blood red? Perhaps a deep maroon?"

I removed my boots and socks, put my feet in the bath water, and tried to relax. At one point I think I started to doze, because all I remember was waking up to a woman crying and screaming.

It was Mary. Her lip was bleeding.

Apparently, I forgot to tell her I was ticklish. That's when I realized I kicked her in the mouth.

With shock, I pointed to Mary and said to my girlfriend, "That's it! That's the color!"

Ψ

Lesson Learned

In any dangerous job, there are risks to be assumed. One shouldn't go on a safari without a gun, one shouldn't clean windows on a skyscraper without a safety wire, and one shouldn't do pedicures on men, least of all, without a wearing a hockey mask. This is just another point in the advocacy for OSHA.

Chucky Choice

On a dark, cold, Thursday night I received a phone call from my girlfriend.

"Hi, sweetie," she said.

"Hi, babe. To what do I owe this honor?" referring, of course, to her phone call.

"Remember how you kept saying you would love to meet my niece and nephews?"

Uh, oh. Kids. A knot formed in my stomach. "Yeah, sure."

"Well you will, honey. Sunday. You and I are taking them to Chuck E. Cheese while my sister and brother-in-law go shopping for a new car."

Holy Crap! You have got to be kidding me. Sunday? This Sunday? Three-days-from-now Sunday? Football day? What the hell did I do to deserve this? No effin' way was I taking three future alcoholics to Chuck E. Cheese. Besides, Chuck E. Cheese doesn't even sell alcohol. Nope. No, siree. That giant freaking mouse would do just fine not seeing my ass at his non-alcoholic establishment.

"Oh, sure, dear," I said. "That'll be fun. What time?" Maybe I could still catch the game.

"We'll all meet there at around noon. They'll drop the kids off with us and then leave. Is that good for you, baby?" she asked.

Noon. Right smack in the middle of the AFC East featured game. Sheesh.

I smiled. "Yeah, that's fine." Yeah, as fine as 40-grit sandpaper.

Sunday rolled around, and I found myself at Chuck E. Cheese about a half hour early. I decided to go in and grab a table. You just never knew how crowded it would be.

I waited in line at the turnstile behind a family with what appeared to me to be ten thousand kids and two parents. What a brood. How did they stay sane? (The kids, not the parents. We already know the parents are insane for coming here in the first place.)

Five minutes and ten thousand three hand-stamps later, I was inside looking for a free table. I would have had better luck finding a Democrat at an NFL Owners meeting.

It was total chaos. There were literally hundreds of unsupervised little people running in all different directions in their socks. It was like a hotel convention of the Lollipop Guild.

Every table I saw had piles of coats, half eaten cold pizza and at least one overweight old lady sitting there making sure no crook stole the game tokens.

Eventually, I pushed my way to the stage area where there were huge mechanical stuffed animals singing god-awful, reworked tunes from the eighties.

This part of Chuck E. Cheese was where most of the big parties were. The tables were set up in long rows, cabaret style, with one party spilling over into the next. It also looked like all the tables were reserved.

Wait! Look over there! People were vacating a booth against the window that, unfortunately, happened to be two rows away. There was a cluster of kids and adults celebrating a birthday between that piece of real estate and me.

Oh no! To the left of that table, I saw a huge woman with a pizza and a balloon making her way towards it. No way was she going to take my table! I saw it first!

I pushed the birthday boy aside, jumped up on their table and ran down the length of tabletops, careful not to step on any cake.

With catlike reflexes, I jumped to a spot devoid of food or presents on the table in the next row, hopped onto the floor and dove into the empty booth. I half expected applause.

Wheezing like a teakettle, I straightened myself up in the seat, smirking over the fact that what I just did was so super cool.

The fat lady with the pizza and balloon looked at me, shook her head, and waddled right by me to sit at the next table with some kids who were already sitting there. Hmmph.

After I caught my breath, I realized that I was stuck to that table like those old ladies I spotted when I came in here. I couldn't get up, I couldn't get a drink, and I couldn't go to the bathroom for fear of losing my table. I was literally in Chuck E. Cheese prison. Instead of stamping hands when you come in the door, they should just issue ankle bracelets.

I looked at my watch. Ten after twelve. I guessed they'd be there any minute. Boy, thinking about not being able to get up made me thirsty and hungry. And now I had to go to the bathroom, too. I wished they would get there soon.

Another twenty minutes passed. Ok, this was just plain crazy. I'd been there almost an hour and no sign of them. Unbelievable. Just think, I could have been in a cozy sports bar watching the Jets kick some ass, but no. I had to be here watching snot bubbles.

I looked at the fat lady with the balloon at the next table. There was a pile of coats and a balloon, but no pizza or kids. I chuckled to myself that maybe she ate them all.

She gave me a dirty look. It was almost as if she read my mind. But, she probably didn't approve of the half gainer I did. Oh, well.

I couldn't tell you how many times I heard very loud women telling their kids, "Eat your pizza, then you'll play." It got on my nerves so badly that I tried to tune it out.

I must've done such a good job of it that I didn't hear my girlfriend calling my name until she was right upon me.

"Oh, hi, honey. What took you so long?" I asked.

"What do you mean what took me so long? We've been waiting for you for forty-five minutes at that table over there."

"You were here?" I ask incredulously. "I've been sitting here for an hour."

She laughed. "Oh that's too funny. Well, come on over to the table, my sister has to get going."

"I have to go there? Why can't you come here?"

"Oh, honey, we've already ordered and the kids are eating." She kissed me on the cheek. "And, I got you a beer, although it's probably warm by now."

"A beer?" I asked. I was shocked. "They serve beer here?"

"Yes, sweetie," she answered. Her smile showed her dimple.

My mood immediately did a one-eighty. "You've got to be kidding. Holy freaking Moly. I had no idea. How cool is that?" Then, in the smoothest way possible, I added, "So, do you come here often?"

My girlfriend giggled and kissed me, again. She turned to leave, gesturing me to follow.

I turned to the fat lady with the balloon and asked, "Do you want my table? I'll give it to you for a beer."

"I wouldn't give you a beer for that table if you danced naked on it at Chippendales."

Whoa. I came to the conclusion that she *did* eat the kids.

Ψ

Lesson Learned

You've worked really hard for (*insert item of choice.*) You're proud of what you've done to get (*insert item of choice.*) And you're proud of how you've acquired (*insert item of choice.*) It's now yours, and nothing or nobody will ever take (*insert item of choice*) away from you. Then your woman appears.

In any given situation, bar none, her (*insert items of her choice*) outweighs your (*insert item of choice*) and, thus, she will force you to give up (*insert item of choice.*)

So, it's your choice whether to just give it up, fight for it, or sell it to a fat woman.

(*Insert correct choice here.*) [HINT: If you don't just give it up, you can be sure that, later at night, she sure as hell won't.

Kneel Diamond

I had it all planned. I had scoped out the place. I had figured out the time. I had done all the research. I knew exactly how I was going to propose to her.

I asked myself, where would the most logical place be for me to ask my girlfriend for her hand in marriage? A marriage is a blessed union between a man and a woman going back centuries to the dawn of man. If you think about Adam and Eve; the apple; the snake; being one with nature—you will probably come to the same conclusion that I did. Yes, it all made sense. There could be no other place to give her the ring. No other place would be more perfect than where nature and man domiciled in one harmonious community; where we could harken back to the days of yore; when life was simple, and all that mankind had was each other. Yes, it was the perfect place. It was the most perfect of all places.

I would ask her to marry me at the zoo.

The perfect time of year to do this was in August, when the sun was shining and the weather was warm. This would give me a few months to plan it.

The next step, and the most important, was the ring. I didn't know that much about diamonds but I kind of knew the shape of the ring she liked. I figured that would be a good start, so I opened up the Sunday paper and looked at all the jeweler advertisements.

When I saw the price of these things I nearly crapped my pants. It certainly looked like I would be selling the old motorcycle to get her a ring. I never rode it anyway (the helmet messed up her hair) so, I figured I could part with it. I also thought that being it was the beginning of riding season, I would get top dollar for it. Maybe someday I'd get another bike, but the ring was the thing that mattered.

Once I sold the bike, I diligently shopped for the best deal. I must have spent hours going from store to store. You get quite an education when you go diamond hunting.

I asked everyone I knew about where to go for a good quality diamond. I got equally as many answers. But, there was this one answer that stood out. A friend of a friend of a cousin of a friend—you get the idea—sent me to a door only accessible from back alley. Once there, an older Asian man would greet me. I should tell him what I wanted and he will find me the perfect diamond. I told my friend I didn't want any stolen merchandise. I was assured the diamonds weren't hot and that I would be getting a fair deal. The Asian man was a jeweler and diamond wholesaler so, I figured, why the hell not?

I found the alley, knocked on the door and met the Asian man. With the greetings and felicitations out of the way, he led me back into his shop and asked me what I wanted.

"I want a one karat emerald cut diamond, preferably a VS2 or higher, with a D or E color," I answered as I looked around making note of the elephant motif in the room.

"I see you are a man who knows what he wants," he said as he removed a soft cloth from his safe.

He laid out a few diamonds, turned on a magnifying elephant lamp, and handed me his jeweler's loupe. I found one I liked, negotiated a price of around $4000 with setting, which took him about 30 minutes or so to put together, and handed the man cash.

"I hope you will be very happy in your marriage, sir," he said as I was walking out.

I turned to him and asked, "Do you have any advice for me?"

"No, I am very sorry, sir. I am in diamond business, not in marriage business. But, I will tell you that in my culture," he waved his hand around the room, "elephants bring luck. Advice to you is always have elephant somewhere near." With that, I left the shop.

I thought, how perfect! With my idea of the zoo and this fellow's superstition of elephants, I took this as some sort of omen. Everything just felt right. I couldn't wait.

August came quickly and I picked the day to take her to the zoo.

I thought about when I was a kid and how I loved Cracker Jack popcorn and peanuts at the ball game. I decided I would put the ring in the Cracker Jack bag as her prize. It was easy to set up when she went to the bathroom.

We strolled over to the elephant area of the zoo. There were two elephants right in our view. It was there I made my move. I handed her the Cracker Jacks.

"No, thanks honey. They hurt my teeth," she said as she pushed them back.

"Come on try some. They're good."

"No, baby, I don't want them."

I was getting nervous now. "Just take a few for me. Please. Besides you may get the prize."

"No, really. I don't want them."

"Baby, you gotta take some." My voice was escalating.

"No, I don't want any." Her voice was escalating, too.

Before we knew it a small crowd started staring at us arguing over the Cracker Jacks. She gets embarrassed easily, so she grabbed the Cracker Jacks from me, took a big scoop with her hand and popped a few caramel popcorn kernels into her mouth.

Suddenly, she stopped chewing and her eyes got wide. I looked to where she was staring and I saw one of the elephants moving his bowels. Imagine that, pooping in front of everyone.

I felt her hand on my shoulder.

"Babe," she said with her mouth full of popcorn.

"I know. You're going to tell me watching elephants take a dump is disgusting."

"No," she mumbled. "I think I broke a tooth."

Oh no! The ring!

Before I could do anything, she walked over to the nearest garbage can and spit out the contents of her mouth.

I leapt at the can, threw the lid down and dumped the contents on the ground. I got on my hands and knees and frantically started rummaging through the garbage looking for the ring.

She stood there laughing.

"What the hell is so funny?" I asked as I continued to look for the ring.

"What are you doing?" she asked in a very calm manner.

I didn't know what to say. I was panicking. Four thousand dollars. I just had to find the ring.

"I'm, uh, looking for something," I replied with sweat from the hot August sun dripping from my brow.

"Could it be you are looking for…"

I turned to her.

"This?" She was pointing to the ring she was holding up.

I jumped up. "The ring! How did you…?"

"You know you can't keep secrets from me," she answered without really answering.

"But, your tooth," I said.

"I faked it. I just wanted to see you panic. So, are you going to ask me or are you just going to stand there with ketchup and burger wrappers in your hand?"

She should have been on the Warren Commission because to this day I don't know how she found out. Or whatever else she faked.

Ψ

Lesson Learned

Apparently, only the elephants that have raised trunks bring good luck, not the ones with upset stomachs. So, you see, there was an omen. I just didn't read it right.

THE WEDDING

My advice to you is to get married. If you find a good wife, you'll be happy; if not, you'll become a philosopher.

~*Socrates*

Piece of Cake

We were all set. We had the wedding date. Now all we needed to do was plan the damn thing.

I always thought that was easy. You pick the hall, the band and the menu, and you are done. My fiancée informed me that I was way off the mark. Every detail takes thought and meticulous scheduling and preparation. She gave me a list.

I read aloud, "Chateau Briand. Pilaf. Coq Au Vin. Grand Marnier Soufflé," I looked up. "So, where are these places?"

"Those aren't places. That's the menu," she corrected.

"Menu? What is all that stuff?"

"Basically steak, rice, chicken with wine, and dessert. It's pronounced soo-flay."

"So, we aren't having burgers and dogs then, I take it." I was disappointed.

"No, dear. This is our wedding. We are doing it right."

By "right" she meant "expensive." My mom used to say, "Beware of women with champagne taste and beer pockets." I never knew what the hell that meant until that day.

"Have we picked the place yet?" I asked her.

"Yes, my mother and I saw this charming hall on the water. This is the menu from that place. We already put a deposit on it."

"Oh, I see. So, are we done?"

"No, silly. We have to order the flowers, pick out the dresses for the brides-maids, pick out the tuxedos, make the invitation list, and of course pick out the invitations."

"Ok. What about the music?"

"Well we have some auditions scheduled with bands that regularly play at the hall we rented. Mom and I are doing that in the next few weeks. We are also debating on whether to have a pianist and harpist or a string quartet for the cocktail hour."

"We're debating that?"

"Yes, my mother and me."

"So, a hip-hop DJ is out of the question?"

"Yes, sweetie," she wrinkled her nose. "We're having live music."

"Oh, I see. So, are we done?"

"No, honey. We need to have the colors picked out. Things shouldn't con-trast with the gowns. We also have to decide on which pastry chef will make the cake. The hall recommended two places, but mom has a friend whose son owns a bakery, so we are going to check that out as well."

"Couldn't we ask the home economics teacher from the local high school to make it? It'd probably be a bit cheaper."

"No, honey," she smirked. "We're having a professionally made wedding cake."

"Oh, I see. So, are we done?"

"No, baby. We need to get prices on the alcohol and champagne. That's probably the most expensive thing on the list. Plus, we need our champagne glasses, you know, the ones you and I will use for our first toast."

"Oh, I see. So, are we done?"

"Not quite. We have to get the videographer and the photographer. Mom and I have a few places scheduled. We just want to see their work before we commit to one."

"We?"

"Mom and I," she nodded.

"Oh, I see. So, are we done?"

"Almost. We need to get gifts for the guests and special gifts for the people in the bridal party."

"Gifts for the guests? I thought we were the ones getting the gifts."

"You always have to give a little remembrance of the wedding, didn't you know that?"

"Uh, oh yeah," I said slapping my forehead. "I just thought that maybe a dent in their wallet when they hand us a check would be enough of a remem-brance."

"Now you're being facetious. There is a lot we have to do." She sighed.

"Yes, I know that," I paused. Then, "So, are we done?"

"Oh!" she exclaimed. "I forgot we have to get a guest book, quill, and cake cutter." Then she thought, "But those things are easy to get. I may even get them in the bridal shower."

"Bridal shower?"

"Yes, baby, a bridal shower. But we don't have to worry about that. The maid of honor takes care of that for me."

"Oh, I see. So, are we done?"

Before she could answer, she looked at her watch, jumped up and said, "Oh, I am going to be late! I have to meet mom and dad. They are taking me shopping for my bridal gown. Gotta run, baby." She kissed me and ran out the door.

See? Nothing to it. Pick the hall, the band and the menu, and you're done.

Ψ

Lesson Learned

You learn, as you go through life, to let the professionals handle the big things. If you need a house, you go to a real estate agent. If you need your appendix removed, you go to a surgeon. If you need a wedding planned, you go to her mother. Then everyone is happy. Your new mother-in-law gets a wedding, your new wife gets marriage, and you get a brand new tax deduction without all the stress.

It's All Gravy

"Come on, we have to go register for the wedding," she said, tugging my arm as we walked through the mall on a beautiful, crisp Saturday afternoon.

"Why do we have to register for the wedding? I never even heard of this before you started bringing home those bridal magazines. Sheesh, those things are the size of phone books."

"Stop joking around. You know very well why we have to register. So we don't get linens in contrasting colors."

"What's wrong with contrasting linens? I'm sure Martha Stewart finds them totally useable."

We walked to the department store and told the customer service girl (who by the way, judging from her braces and boyish figure, couldn't be older than fourteen) that we were getting married and needed to register.

I joked to the salesgirl that getting married was a lot like buying a car—you needed a license, you picked a color, you picked a place to get it, and you registered. The only thing different is that they did away with the inspection. You could marry whomever you want to destroy your life, finances, and sanity, but god forbid you have a taillight out. The girl didn't seem to get it. I guess she wasn't old enough to drive.

Come to think of it, my fiancée wasn't too thrilled with the joke, either.

The girl handed us a contraption with a keypad on it and a trigger. She explained that when we found an item we wanted, we should hold this thing up to the barcode and pull the trigger. It would then put that information into a database so that everyone would know exactly what we want. This piece of technological wizardry was roughly the size of a brick and twice as heavy.

I figured I would try another joke, being that the first one bombed and all. I held the scanner up to my ear and feigned horror. "You're kidding? Oh, no! Reagan's been shot!"

"That's not funny," my fiancée chastised. "You are just making fun of my father."

"I am not," I protested.

I made a futile attempt at trying to explain the joke. "It was just that this thing looked like an old cell phone. I meant it as to date it back in the eighties. Get it?"

I turned to the salesgirl with outstretched hands, "You get it, don't you?"

"I, like, kind of get it. Like, you want to have a date with the phone, like, 'cause you're getting married and you feel like your life is over and your car, like, has no brake lights. Am I right?"

Did you ever have one of those days where you reached for the Tylenol and prayed somebody had tampered with it?

I turned to my fiancée and said, "You, see? She gets it." I then put down the barcode reader and walked off to the electronics section.

She followed. "What are you doing? We need to pick out items for the registry."

"I am. I'm picking out a new big screen TV."

"We don't need a big screen TV. Besides, nobody is going to buy us such an expensive gift." She grabbed my hand. "Come on, sweetheart. Let's do this together. It'll be fun, and then we can go home and relax."

"Ok," I relented, and off we went to the housewares section. (Not getting a bigger TV turned out to be a grave mistake. See the chapter titled *Don't Suet It.*)

About a half hour into it, she was blazing up and down the aisles zapping every bar code in sight. "Hey, babe?" I cleared my throat. "I thought you said we would be doing this together."

"We are, honey. I just thought that it would go faster if I picked out the things that I really care about."

"I just thought that maybe I would be included in picking out this stuff, too. I mean, I am going to have to live with it, too, right?"

She stopped and let out a breath. "Yes, dear, you're right. Come here. Tell me which one of these you prefer."

"Uh, what is it?"

"It's a gravy boat."

"What the hell is a gravy boat?"

"It's an elegant way of pouring gravy on your dinner. It eliminates having to use a ladle."

"What the hell is a ladle?"

"Uh, honey, is there a game on TV today?"

"Ok, I get you. I'll be over in the electronics section if you want me."

Ψ

Lesson Learned

Always make an attempt to do the things she wants to do. And if you do them with the utmost ignorance, you never have to worry about missing the boat.

PUShiNG Their BUttONs

"Are you ready to go, yet?" she asked with a slight annoyance to her tone. She always hates to be late anywhere. I suppose that's a good thing.

"Yes, dear, in a second," I answered, thinking of how many thousands of times I would say that over the course of my life.

I quickly rummaged through a drawer to find the item I was looking for. I grabbed it, put it in my jacket pocket, and off we went to our rehearsal dinner.

While en route to the hall, I broke the silence. "Why do we have to practice the wedding?"

"It's tradition. It's also so we know where we will stand, what will be said and how everything will flow."

"How hard could it be? You come down the aisle holding up your father and I slap a ring on your hand."

"Is everything a joke with you?"

"Come on, I'm just trying to make you smile," I lied. Then I asked, "So, how long is this going to take?"

She sighed. "It won't take long. We'll rehearse and then go to dinner, ok?"

"Yes, dear."

We arrived at the hall just a bit late and she made sure to let me know it was my fault. Her mother was there as well as all the people in the bridal party. The minister was notably missing, as was her father.

"They were both here a couple of minutes ago. I don't know where they went," explained her mother.

"Probably to the nearest bar," I mumbled. It turned out I wasn't that far off.

When we decided to get married, we knew we needed someone to preside over the ceremony. Although my fiancée's parents were Catholic, we opted for a civil ceremony because neither of us was very religious. Rather than do it in a courthouse, we decided to enlist a non-denominational minister to be the one to marry us. And when we mentioned this to her parents her dad piped up with this guy, a friend of his. This may have explained why he wasn't too upset we weren't having a religious ceremony. Her father is such a tightwad I wouldn't be surprised if he got a kickback from our hiring his minister friend.

The minister, Isaac Blear, went by the moniker of Reverend Ike. Apparently, Reverend Ike and her dad, as I found out a few weeks prior, met during a beer chugging contest at an Oktoberfest celebration in Bartolec's Tavern some years back. They hit it off and had been friends ever since. Now, I was getting married by my future father-in-law's drinking buddy. Go figure.

"Oh, there they are," pointed one of the bridesmaids. Her name was Battie, or Cattie, or Fattie; something like that. I could never remember, although that last one fit her to a tee. It was a good thing the gowns were black.

I reached into my pocket and took out the little round disc I had found in the drawer earlier and put it on my lapel.

Reverend Ike took out his book of notes and proceeded to tell us the agenda of the ceremony. I would stand on his left with my best man while her dad walked her up the aisle. He would say some nice poetic thing, we would exchange vows, I would place the ring on her finger, and "Pow!" (his words) we were married.

When Ike said "Pow!" I felt like passing out. He had leaned into me and his breath damn near knocked me down. I knew it! Ike and her dad were out boozing it up—and on the eve of my wedding, too! And to think the bastards never once thought to invite me.

Reverend Ike waved his hand and motioned my fiancée and her dad to walk up the aisle. Her dad let go of her arm as she took her place next to me.

She looked so lovely. She was smiling and I could tell she was just on cloud nine. She turned her head to look at me and that's when she saw it. That smile turned upside down in a hurry.

"What the hell is that?"

"What?"

"That," she said pointing to the button on my lapel.

"Nothing," I replied as I darted my eyes left and right.

Reverend Ike, already inebriated and teetering on the stair in front of us, leaned in to take a look. He blinked his eyes and tried to focus them on my chest. He leaned in a little closer. His face got beet red and although everyone later blamed my lapel pin and me for his slipping off the step, I'm pretty sure he passed out long before he hit the floor.

Women screamed. Commotion followed. People asked if he had a heart attack. Her dad was telling everybody to get back and give him some air. I quietly stepped aside and slowly made my way to the back of the room. My best man followed.

"What did you do?" he asked me.

I showed him the button on my lapel.

He read it and smiled. "That's pretty funny. It's cool how you managed to get two birds with one stone, making fun of both Ike and her dad. Very subtle. It's almost genius." He leaned in, "But you know you're going to pay for that."

I shrugged my shoulders. "I'm already paying for the whole damn wedding, I might as well get my kicks."

He shook his head and chuckled. "Where did you ever get an 'All The Way With Adlai' button, anyway?"

Ψ

Lesson Learned

If you know you are going to do something that will upset your woman, you better be sure it's worth all the trouble. It is the Butch Cassidy and The Sundance Kid tactic: You know you're going down, so you better take out as many of them as you can.

RiGht On Track

The doorbell rang. "Jut a second," I yelled as I was straightening my bowtie in the mirror. Man, my collar was killing me. I didn't think razor burn and a starched shirt went together.

I walked to the door and opened it. An older guy in a dark suit was standing there.

"Hello, sir. I'm Charles, your driver today. I will wait outside in the car. Take your time. Come out whenever you're ready." He turned and walked back to his car.

"Thanks, I'll be just a minute." This was going to be my first ride in a limousine. I should have been stoked, but I was more numb than anything. There was something incredibly morbid about the day, my wedding day.

Why is it that the two times in an average person's life when he rides in a limousine, he is only alive for one? As a matter of fact, I think that the whole ceremony of marriage parallels that of death.

Take the suit, for instance. You get dressed up in your best clothes for both. The only difference is, for the wedding it's rented. I suppose it could be rented for death, too, but the late fees would be so enormous it wouldn't pay.

You walk down the aisle for the wedding; you walk down a tunnel when you die. Only for the wedding, there is dark at the end of the aisle.

In death, you meet your maker. In life you make her after you meet her.

In death, there will be no more hanging out with the guys, no watching football all winter, no getting drunk at a tittie bar, no buying expensive electronics on a whim, no blowing a whole month's pay at the track. In marriage...Uh, well, you get my point.

So, if the Grim Reaper won't allow all those things, and the wife won't allow all those things, then ipso facto, the wife must be Satan.* That's to say nothing of Satan's mother. I don't even want to broach that subject.

I must have been losing my mind. I should have been looking at it like it was the best, most joyous day of my life. Instead, I was looking at it like it was Mount Vesuvius and I was working late as a claims adjuster for Pompeii Life and Casualty.

Then something snapped in my head. It was like I'd had an epiphany. I looked at my watch. It was noon. The wedding started at four o'clock. Plenty of time, I thought.

I walked out to the car. Charles opened the door for me. I climbed in the back, and then Charles got in the front and started to drive away.

Charles started to make small talk. "So, are you ready for the big day, sir?"

I ignored his question. "Hey, uh, Charlie," I said as I cleared my throat.

"Yes, sir," he said inquisitively as he looked in the mirror.

"I want to make a quick stop before we get to the hall." I then told him where I wanted to go.

"Very good, sir." I noticed him smirking in the mirror.

About an hour later we arrived at the destination. I leaned over the front seat and said, "Just go to valet parking. You're coming with me."

Ten minutes later we were in the Grandstands poring over the racing form.

"Who do you have in the third?" I asked Charlie.

"I like Mighty Like Earl. He's 6 to 1."

"Good choice. I'll go with that. Here's a twenty. You put it to win and I'll go get us a couple of dogs and beer and I'll meet you right back here."

His face lit up with a big smile. "Very good, sir," he said as he walked away.

Before I could say, "Stop with the 'very good, sir' crap," two very attractive young women came up to me.

"Hi, my name is Christy and this is my friend Shawn. You seem to know a lot about racing. Could you give us a few tips?"

It never fails. I spent my entire adult life praying for a moment like this, and it had to come on today of all days. I could be arrogant about it, but we all know it was because I was in a tuxedo at the racetrack. They must have thought I was a spy. Chicks dig that. Yep, that was me. A fat James Bond. All right. I'd play their little game.

---

* The wife is only Satan if the dead man is going to Hell. Since most men think marriage is Hell, Satan would be the correct choice for this comparison.

"Well, Christy and Shawn, I actually have amassed my fortune playing the ponies. As a matter of fact, I own a horse that is racing in the next race." I looked down at the racing form and picked a random horse.

"Secretariat Spread. He's at 9 to 1, but what everybody doesn't know," I leaned in closer and whispered, "is that the jockey will be switched at the last minute with Herve Villachez. Smart money will put him to place." I winked at them. "Hurry up and go bet before they close the window."

Like two schoolgirls they thanked me and ran off to the betting window. My eyes followed them both as they bounced away.

I sighed and went to get the food.

We had a nice couple of hours, old Charlie and me. But then it was time to get to the hall and get married.

When we arrived at a quarter to four, her mother was in an absolute tizzy. She ranted about my being late and how the photographer wanted to take pictures of the groom's side, and how everybody was worrying.

"Where were you? Why are you so late? Do you know that the Reverend has another wedding at five o'clock?" She just bombarded me with questions.

"Relax," I said holding up my hands, trying to calm her down. "It's not even four yet. I'm here and we still have a few minutes. We can always take the photos after the ceremony."

"Well, why are you so late?" she persisted.

"Sheesh. I just needed a little time to get ready, that's all. It's my wedding day, for crying out loud. Where do you think I've been, at the racetrack?"

Ψ

Lesson Learned

You must take time to do the things that make you happy, even if other people might not approve. And you must never, ever lie about it. Just make whatever you did sound like the most absurd thing and they will leave you alone. Plus, if you ever have to take a lie detector test, you will pass. That is, unless Christy and Shawn administer the test.

I DID?

Well, there we were. I was standing next to my best man. We were both in front of Reverend Ike listening to the *Wedding March*.

I was staring at Reverend Ike's sling. That was going to look real peachy in the wedding album. He had dislocated his shoulder in the fall the night before, but I was pretty sure he was so plastered he didn't feel a thing.

I was feeling a bit numb. It was almost as if I was having an out-of-body experience. I think I was sweating, but I really wasn't sure.

I was also incredibly aware that I had a tongue. I started using it to feel my molars and the ridges on the roof of my mouth. Then I started twisting it around itself inside of my mouth. Hey, it had been a while since I tried to touch my nose with my tongue. I think I was a kid the last time I even thought about that. I wondered if I could still do it. I thought I'd try it.

Before I knew it the music stopped, my bride was standing next to me, and everyone was fixated on me craning my neck trying to touch my nose with my tongue.

I looked around, cleared my throat, and nodded to Ike. "Proceed."

Ike started with the standard, "Dearly beloved…" Boy was this cliché.

I knew he was talking but I really wasn't paying attention.

I can't believe I am actually standing here getting married. Me. Married. Unbelievable. Marriage. My marriage.

Marriage, marriage, marriage. Hey, if you rearrange the letters in "marriage," it comes out "a grim era." Ha! How's that for irony? Let's see what other anagrams

I could come up with. Hmmm…"I love weddings" rearranges to…let me think…Holy crap! "God, devil swine!"

Just then, my best man kicked me. I looked at him, "What the hell did you do that for…?" I was staring at his hand holding the wedding ring, right in the face.

I cleared my throat again, took the ring, held it out, and faced Ike.

"Hey, schmuck," my best man whispered. And, quite loudly, I might add. "You're not marrying Ike. It goes on the bride's finger."

I looked over at my beautiful bride. I let out a sigh.

My beautiful bride.

She looked so beautiful, with that beautiful dress.

And that beautiful veil.

And that beautiful frown.

I looked up at Ike for guidance.

"Place the ring on her finger and repeat after me. I, Larry…"

Oh, Jeez! It's really happening! I, Larry, take whatshername to be my blah, blah, blah. Uh, oh. Here comes that damn question. Do you promise…? How the hell did I get in this mess? It feels like the walls are closing in around me. All I hear is my heart beating. I wonder if anyone else could hear it. Oh, no. I have to answer now, dammit. I dread saying these words just as sure as I hate purchasing feminine products. Oh, well. Deep breath. Here goes nothing.

"I do."

Now, I was sure I was sweating. I was sweating so profusely that I was dripping perspiration on her hand. That was ok though, because it helped the ring slide on better.

She said her vow without hesitation. Each of us now sported a band of gold. That ring represented that union of marriage of which there was no inexpensive escape.

All in all, it wasn't so bad, although I did feel a bit drained. My stomach was a bit queasy, but I guessed I'd be ok. I had so much anxiety. I was just glad it was over. I wiped my forehead with my sleeve and looked at Ike for his final words.

"Marriage," he said with outstretched hands. "Is a lot like bungee jumping for the first time."

Huh? You been sucking on that rum candy again?

"You know you want to do it; you make the arrangements and prepare yourself as best you can. But you are never fully prepared when you take that initial plunge. You think you are, but you are not. It's frightening and exhilarating all at the same time. And when it's finally over, you have a feeling and a memory that will last a lifetime. But, just remember, it's not as much fun the second time around."

Trust me, Ike. It wasn't fun the first time.

Ψ

Lesson Learned

Ike was close in his analogy. It's not that marriage is like bungee *jumping*, it's that marriage is like the bungee *itself*; that huge rubber cord that bounces you over Death's mouth. Your marriage is solely dependent upon that rubber. And if you don't use one, you will have a few little bungee jumpers flinging themselves around your house before you are prepared for it.

Turn On The Blinkers

We took a cruise to the Caribbean for our honeymoon. We were only going to be gone for a week, but she packed enough things for nuclear fallout. I had one carry-on consisting of 2 pairs of pants, 2 pairs of underwear (there were laundry facilities on the boat, so don't get grossed out), 2 shirts, 1 pair of dress shoes, swimming trunks and a toothbrush. The customary toiletries were provided in the stateroom (see the chapter titled *The Beach Is Back* for my introduction into her world of cosmetics).

She, on the other hand, had two rather hefty suitcases, her everyday purse, and a makeup case the size of an old Vaudevillian steamer trunk, which I affectionately referred to as "The Crate."

She spent the first evening on the ship unpacking. I had made a couple of laps around the deck, checked out the dining facilities, had a drink as I was looking over the port bow, and came back to the room finding her unpacking the same case she was unpacking when I left.

"Why must you bring so much?" I queried.

"It's not so much," she answered on her knees with her face buried in The Crate.

I blinked my eyes rapidly.

"Not so much?" I asked, incredulously. "They had to give us a room amidships so the damn boat wouldn't list."

She proceeded to mumble something about not having some kind of lipstick color and then got up and dragged The Crate into the bathroom.

"I'll be on deck by the pool when you're done moving in." I turned and walked out.

There I was on the chaise lounge, three sheets to the wind, smoking a cigar, when she strolled up. "Hi, honey. What kept you?" I asked, posting a damn goofy smile.

"Very funny. I finally got everything situated, no thanks to you. Do you know how small the vanity is in our bathroom? It's a wonder I fit everything on there. Good thing there was a hook on the bathroom door." She paused for a second and then said, "I am so famished. Are you ready for dinner?"

I blinked my eyes as rapidly as I could, given my slightly inebriated state. "Nope, I drank my dinner three hours ago waiting for you. It's almost midnight. With how long you were taking, I figured you were wallpapering the stateroom. Did you bring enough glue? 'Cause if you didn't I'm sure Captain Stubing over there will be happy to mix some flour and water for you."

"Can you tell me why you are so sarcastic? Don't make me sorry I married you," she retorted.

"I'm sorry, honey. It's just that I didn't think I would be spending our first night onboard, alone. I'm not feeling too well, though. I think I'm going to go to bed. Tomorrow we'll start fresh, ok?" I got up from the chaise lounge after the third try, kissed her on the cheek, and stumbled down the deck.

By morning, I felt fine. No noticeable hangover; just a taste of, what I could only describe as, carbonated manure. I got out of bed and went into the bathroom to brush my fuzzy teeth.

I stood there for a few minutes looking for the sink, until I realized it was buried under all those colorful little bottles, tubes, and containers.

Another few minutes went by until I finally found my toothbrush. It was nestled between a toe callous softener and a squeeze tube of something called "The Ultimate Firming Masque." (Five hours later that day, it hit me—she had alphabetized the freaking sundries.)

I finished brushing my teeth, pushed aside some pencils and skin brightening gel, and put down my toothbrush. I grabbed a ship-supplied towel and got ready for my shower. I closed the bathroom door and went to hang the towel on the door hook. That's when I saw it.

Unfurled and hanging from the door hook was this toiletries case that was reminiscent of a WWII body bag. There had to be 10 different shampoos, 12 kinds of conditioners and toners, an overabundance of scissors, clamps and clips, and enough sponges, crumpled nets and loufahs to cushion a Space Shuttle landing.

I blinked my eyes rapidly.

It was at that point I seriously thought that this woman I married was, totally and unequivocally, insane.

After my shower, I felt much less tense and more relaxed. My new bride went into the bathroom as I was getting my legs into one of two pair of pants I plucked out of my carry-on. I heard mumbling emanating from the bathroom. It was low and indiscernible, but I had the feeling it was directed toward me. I feverishly thought back on what I could have done, but nothing came to mind. Then I heard cabinet doors bang closed. I also heard some bottles or something slam down on the sink. The mumbling and noises grew louder.

Beads of sweat formed on my brow.

The bathroom door opened and her voice bellowed throughout the cabin—"How am I supposed to find anything when you leave your toothbrush lying around all over the place!"

I blinked my eyes rapidly.

Ψ

Lesson Learned

Make sure when you get married you know of all the little quirks beforehand, e.g. alphabetizing bathroom items on vacation. Also make sure you have the wherewithal to tolerate them for the rest of your life. Otherwise, it will sure as hell drive you to blink.

THE MARRIAGE

They say marriages are made in Heaven. But so is thunder and lightning.

~Clint Eastwood

we Kneaded It

There comes a time in every American middle class couple's life when the wife goes to the husband and says, "I've decided I'm going to massage therapy school."

"Well, that's great, honey," you reply, but your blood is boiling. You are still paying off hairdresser school, dental technician school, and veterinary assistant school. You politely ask about each of the other courses she failed to complete, and she has a plausible answer for each. The hair chemicals give her a headache; looking in people's mouths just makes her retch; and the only job she could find as a vet assistant was for $5.50 per hour cleaning the kennel in the local Pooch Hotel. No, this time she assures you it is something she is going to see through to the end. There is a lot of money to be made in massage therapy.

Your mind races: *Massage therapy. Massage freaking therapy. Correct me if I'm wrong, but doesn't that entail touching people and rubbing them into sheer and utter ecstasy? How about touching your husband and rubbing him into sheer and utter ecstasy, huh? You haven't touched me since the Rams won the Super Bowl. It would be nice to have you freaking massage me for a while—after all I'm the one paying for all your whims. Whenever you get a bug up your ass to start doing something to give us an extra income, it costs me more freaking money and aggravation than it's worth. You want to massage something? Get in the freaking kitchen and massage that ground beef into a meatloaf.*

You say: "Sounds like a sound investment in our future. To whom do I make the check?"

You find out she will be at class Tuesday and Thursday night. Let's see…Monday night you have Monday Night Football with the boys, Tuesday night she is at class, Wednesday she gets her hair and nails done all day, Thursday night she's at class. Weekends are a crapshoot. So, that leaves Friday as the only night during the week that you know you will be together. Sounds good to you.

When my wife was four weeks into her nine-month course, she told me that they were going to work in groups. Massaging in groups? What the hell was that all about? Was the Democratic convention coming to town? I don't mind telling you that I was becoming a bit uncomfortable with this whole thing.

I had the idea that maybe I would take a class, too. Maybe something to get my mind off of her massage therapy school. I figure if she could do it, then so could I. So, I brought it up to her on one Friday night.

"Well, I think that's a wonderful idea. There are a lot of classes that you can take like some business classes, or computer classes. I'm sure you'll find something."

Wow. I was taken aback by her encouragement. Maybe this massage school was a good idea after all.

I perused the local community college adult education newsletter. The headings were quite banal: Learn Guitar. Introduction to Letter Writing. Buy a Foreclosed Property with No Money Down. I was getting ready to put the paper down when I saw it. Right there between Presenting Like a Pro and Hula Dancing for Fun. It was Pie Making 101. To some people this might sound ridiculous. Why would I want to go to a pie making class? To me the answer was obvious.

By going to massage therapy school, my wife was doing something that I was not at all too happy about, so I figured turn-about was fair play. In my childish way, I needed to make my wife feel as uncomfortable as I felt.

How would my going to a pie making class make her feel uncomfortable?

Simple. Your first thought probably is that if she tells people her husband is taking a pie making class she would appear as if she married a man who is not quite in touch with his masculine side; someone who may be a tad too submissive. This would make her look like a dominating woman; headstrong and not easy to get along with (which really wouldn't be that far from the truth). Therefore, her classmates would want to steer clear of her. If her classmates steer clear of her, she won't be able to do the "group lab work" required. This would result in an "F" and she will fail. While this may be a malicious and highly improbable benefit to my taking the pie course, the reality of it was that the pie class would be full of women. Women who like to cook. Women who want to bake pies to make their husbands fat and happy.

The next Tuesday night, my wife informed me that she was quitting the massage therapy class. She cited her having to shorten her nails as the reason.

"That's too bad, baby," I said.

"Well, I'm free now on Tuesday and Thursday nights. Do you want to do something Thursday?" she asked.

"Sorry, I can't. I have to practice making a lattice crust."

Ψ

Lesson Learned

The old saying an eye for an eye may be valid in this instance. But don't take out too many eyes or you won't be able to see exactly whose pie you both are massaging.

Move Over, Por Favor

A few years into our marriage we finally saved up enough money and vacation time to take the trip we always wanted—two weeks in fabulous Cancun, Mexico in a five star hotel and the timing couldn't be better. We were kind of losing touch with one another and this offered us the perfect opportunity to rekindle that flame of love that I felt needed stoking.

The last long trip we had gone on was our honeymoon (see the chapter titled *Turn On The Blinkers*). While that trip was fun, it was pretty confining because we spent most of our time being held by the cruise line's schedule. We decided to plan this trip to Cancun in a more free flowing fashion; that is to say there would be no planning. There would be no schedule to which we would adhere. We would do whatever we wanted to do, whenever we wanted to do it. Time was of no consequence except, of course, catching the flights.

Three weeks before we were scheduled to leave, my wife came to me with what she called "wonderful news about our trip."

"Oh, really?" I asked, genuinely interested. I was excited to see her share my desire for our little romantic getaway. "What is it, baby?"

"My parents said they want to come with us to Cancun."

My brain instantly went on red alert.

Are you out of your freaking mind? What the hell are you thinking? This was supposed to be our just-the-two-of-us-getting-the-passion-back-in-our-marriage vacation in Cancun, not take Gomez and Morticia to Disneyland. This is crazy, just freaking crazy.

I worked myself up into a frenzy. I knew I had to calm down, so I took a deep breath.

Let me just try to think this through logically and soundly, without all this emotion. Maybe she told them no. Maybe she is just saying this conversationally in passing. Yeah, that's it. I would like to think I know my wife. Sure, that's it. My wife would tell them no. I just know she would. There, I feel better.

"Well, what did you say?" I asked as calmly as I could.

"I told them I would ask you"

I knew it. I knew she wouldn't tell them no. Great. Just great. Leave me with the decision. If I say no, I look like the bad guy and I'd probably fight with her for the three weeks leading up to the trip, the two weeks during the trip and the 35 years after the trip. I just have to think of a graceful way out of it. Come on, think man. Think!

I got it.

"Well, babe, we already paid for the trip and it is non-refundable. You know I would if I could, but we really can't afford to re-book the whole vacation."

There. That should quell any sort of rebuttal.

"Tell your parents that I'm really sorry."

"I thought of that, too," she replied.

I let out an audible sigh. *Good. Catastrophe averted.*

Then she added, "But, the sister of mom's hairdresser is a travel agent and she offered to downgrade the hotel and book the extra flights. The whole thing, with the penalty of canceling the hotel reservations, would only cost us $200.00 more. Dad said he would pay the difference."

He would pay the difference? He still owes me $1200.00 for your damn wedding dress. That man hasn't paid for anything since the Eisenhower administration. I had never met a cheaper man in all my life. If he pinched his nickels any tighter the damn buffalo would look like roadkill. If I am any judge of character, that man won't part with a dime. That, in a nutshell, would be my only saving grace.

"Sure, if he wants to pay for it," I told her.

"Good, because that's what I told them you would say. Do I know my husband or what? I gave mom your credit card and dad will just pay us back when the bill comes in." She gave me a kiss and walked out of the room.

I do believe I was hornswoggled. Again.

Ψ

Lesson Learned

You spend years living with someone. You learn their habits. You learn their shortcomings. You study their movements, tastes, and mannerisms. You're waking hours are spent mulling over their decisions, both good and bad. You analyze their thought processes and their inconsistencies. You have never second-guessed their actions because you know your first thoughts about them were correct. You live and breathe their very essence as if it were your own. You think you know a person backwards and forwards. And then you find out—she certainly does.

Dog Day Afternoon

"What are you doing today?" she asked.

I picked my head up from a pillow on the sofa. "You're looking at it."

"Come on, honey, you do that every Saturday. Today I need a favor."

My eyes rolled. "What favor?"

"I promised Grandma I would take her to the vet."

"Can't she use a doctor like a normal human?"

She sighed and gave me one of those looks that said, "So, you're the one that farted in the elevator."

"No," she said with her jaw jutting. "One of her cats has a bladder infection and I promised I would take her, but I also promised Wendy I would go with her to get her hair done."

"Wendy?"

"Yes, my friend Wendy. You met her before."

I thought for a moment. How could I forget her? "Oh, you mean Tubya. Yes, I remember her."

"Why must you be so mean? You aren't exactly slim yourself."

"I never said I was, but I don't have dimples in my ass big enough to put my fist in, either. What exactly do you want from me?"

"I need you to take Grandma and Blackie to the vet, while I take Wendy to the salon. Their appointments are for the same time."

"Why can't you just change the time?" This seemed like a logical question to me.

She took a deep breath. "It took two weeks to get a Saturday appointment and Wendy can't get a baby sitter, so I have to watch Hayden while she gets it done."

I started laughing.

"What's so funny?" she asked as she placed her hands on her hips.

"I was just thinking, Hayden and the Planetarium."

"You can be a real jerk, sometimes, Larry."

I wiped the corner of my eye. "Ok, ok. I'll watch Hayden. How old is he, seven? Eight?"

"He's eighteen months."

"Right." I thought it over for a second. "I'll watch Grandma. Her I can catch."

"Thank you very much," she said, enunciating every word. "Here are the directions. Her appointment is at two." She handed me a piece of paper, threw her purse over her shoulder, and walked out the door.

I got up, got dressed, made some coffee and went to pick up Grandma in my truck.

On the way over I actually thought about putting a bandana around my mouth and nose so I wouldn't have to smell the stench when I walked through her door, but I figured she would think it was a stickup. But, that turned out to be moot because she was waiting outside with Blackie in some kind of carrier. Thank heavens for small miracles.

"Hi, Grandma. Let me take that," I said as I grabbed the carrier. "Funny, this thing looks like my lunch box."

"No, I haven't had lunch, yet. I've been too worried about Blackie," she replied. I could see this was going to be fun.

I opened the passenger door of the pick-up and put Blackie in the cab behind the passenger seat, but I had a sneaking suspicion that Grandma wasn't going to be able to get in quite as easily.

The truck was way too tall for her diminutive, frail body to climb up, so I reached around Grandma's back and hoisted her up by her armpits, praying to God that I don't, A, drop her, or B, feel her tits.

Remember a second ago when I thanked the heavens for small miracles? I take that back, because out of nowhere this dog comes charging right at us, barking and showing it's teeth. Blackie is having a heart attack, hissing and fogging up the carrier, and this dog is snapping at my feet with me holding Grandma a good three feet off the ground. I'm swinging Grandma around like she was Tai Babilonia going for the Olympic gold.

I panicked. This dog was now desperately trying to dig its teeth into my ass. I was trying to push it away with my foot while still clutching Grandma, hoping to keep her out of harm's way. I felt I was going to trip and any moment Grandma and I would be rolling around in the gutter between the curb and the truck with the dog's jaw firmly clamped on my genitals. I did the only thing I could do given the immediacy of the situation. I threw Grandma face down on the seat and jumped in the bed of my truck.

This guy ran down the street screaming at the dog. Apparently, he was the dog's owner because the beast put his tail between its legs and cowered down when he reached us.

After a few minutes of his apologizing for the dog's frightening me like that, and his reassurance that I wouldn't wind up as his chew toy, I climbed out of the bed and went immediately to Grandma.

She was lying face down on the front passenger seat, hanging halfway out of the truck with her legs dangling out of the open door. Her right shoe was in the middle of the street, apparently kicked by me in the scuffle, and about 18 inches of stocking was flapping in the breeze off the end of her exposed foot.

"Grandma, are you alright? Please tell me you're alright." I was breathing very hard.

"I see you met Max," she said softly, resting her cheek on the center armrest.

"Max? The dog? You know this dog?"

"Yes. He lives two houses down. He comes by to visit every now and then, especially when I make a beef stock. I give him the bones. How he loves the bones."

"You've got to be kidding me." I turned to the dog's owner, "So, why did he attack her if he's so friendly?"

"He didn't attack her. He attacked you. He thought you were trying to hurt her when you picked her up," he answered.

I lashed out. "Well, you should have that mongrel on a leash. He's a menace. Somebody could've gotten seriously hurt."

"Larry, darling," called Grandma, her blue hair still smashed in the seat cushion. "I think we better get going or we'll be late for the vet appointment."

"Ok," I sighed. I looked down at Max and then at his owner. "Well, are you going to help her down or what?"

"Me?"

"Yes, you." I pointed to the dog, "I don't want McGruff here thinking I'm crime, you know what I mean? So, you are going to have to help her down."

He relented and I went off to retrieve her shoe from the middle of the street. Just then I heard more barking and growling.

I ran back to the truck in time to see Max chasing his owner down the block. Grandma was standing on the curb fixing her stockings.

"Good for him," I said watching them disappear down the block. "That was freaking horrifying. I hope he gets his just desserts." I handed Grandma her shoe.

She patted my face with a wrinkled hand. "I already told you, darling, I can't eat. I'm too worried about Blackie."

I should've watched Hayden.

Ψ

Lesson Learned

You will find out sooner or later that in life what seems to be the easiest choice isn't necessarily the best choice, and vice versa. What may look hard on the surface could very well wind up being a piece of cake. That is, unless you're too worried to eat.

A Few Things I Can
Live Without

Here are a few peeves of mine.

1. Toilet seat lid covers: If you ever see one of these in a house, you know it was put there by a woman. These badly colored, furry bathroom accoutrements are the cause of almost every man's bathroom woes and subsequent arguments.

We've all heard the questions from our significant others: Why does it smell like a public restroom in here? Why can't you aim? Why do you have to pee on the floor? Well, ladies, here is your answer. Get rid of the damn lid covers and you will eliminate 80 percent of your problem with men and their urination.

You see, the lid never stays up when you have the cover on it, so a man has to be an acrobat, standing on the side of the bowl, holding it up with one knee, while trying to drain his bladder into the toilet.

Sometimes men don't think about the lid cover and the havoc it can cause, especially when he is in someone else's home. A man will walk up to the front of the toilet, lift the lid and the seat and then start to do his business. But before he finishes, the lid will come crashing down, snapping at his groin like a porcelain wide mouth bass after a tasty treat.

Naturally, he finds it difficult to stop mid stream and thus continues to urinate onto a closed toilet. He spends the next twenty minutes trying to clean up his mess, usually with toilet paper because he will hear a mouthful from the old lady if he dirties the show towels.

With all his trying, he never manages to get the urine out of the toilet seat lid cover, so he leaves it, hoping it will dry before anyone will notice.

He will exit the bathroom with that cat-that-swallowed-the-canary look on his face, only to hear that dreaded mandatory question: What did you do, fall in?

2. Father-in-law's advice: I don't mind advice from anyone, especially if they have been down a path that I have yet to travel. But when I have to get advice that I have to decipher, it frustrates me as much as taking the cellophane off of a new DVD. When I got married, my then brand-new father-in-law came over to me drink in hand and told me he wanted to give me advice about my marriage. He held up his finger and said, "I want to say one word to you. Just one word."

I was intrigued. This is cool—advice from my new Daddy. What could it be? "Ok, shoot."

"Are you listening to me?"

"Yes, I am. Intently, I might add."

He took a sip of his highball, leaned in and said, "Plastics."

"Plastics?" I asked.

He nodded. "Plastics."

He patted me on the back and walked away.

Sometime later that evening, he blessed me with more of his cryptic advice. He approached me, looked at me with his half-lidded bloodshot eyes, teetered for a second and said, "It's very comfortable just to drift here."

I looked at him and could think of nothing to do but agree. "Yes. Yes, it is." I darted my eyes from side to side and then added, "I think I'm just going to drift over there to the band. You can continue just to drift here, ok?"

I thought about his words a lot. They weighed heavily on my soul. I needed insight. I needed guidance. I had no idea what the hell he was trying to tell me. That is until two months later when I was watching American Movie Classics and realized he was quoting lines from the freaking Graduate.

3. Bulk Buying: You know those big chain stores that sell everything cheaper than every place else? Great idea, right? Sure. Only there is a catch. You have to buy a thousand pieces to get the low per item price.

Can someone tell me what the purpose of this is? Do I really need enough coffee filters to last me until I get my AARP card? What am I going to do with ten pounds of mayonnaise? Why does my wife insist on buying 144 cans of peas? I hate peas.

I can't tell you how many times I've carted the same box of plastic knives from one apartment to another. She had to have them for her cousin's baby shower. The kid is starting college now.

They never even got used. The box was still closed when we brought them home. Did she return them? No, of course not. "We will surely need them," she'd say. "They're good to have in a pinch," she'd say. What pinch? How many times in my life will I be pinched to use 500 plastic knives?

A day or two after the last time we moved, mostly all the kitchen stuff was still in boxes. I wanted a sandwich but I couldn't find the box with the utensils. I knew where that box of plastic knives was, so I opened that and used a knife to spread some of the ten pounds of mayonnaise we had on my bread. Then I tossed the knife in the sink. She came over to me, put her hands on her hips and said, "Why are you wasting those knives? We have knives that you could use, you didn't need to use the plastic ones."

Sheesh! The way she was acting you would think I just changed my truck's oil on the beach.

Although it took me a few hours, I got even with her the next night. When she was asleep, I went outside and put my plan into action.

In our apartment complex, strips of grass separate the parking spots. I took the 499 knives and stuck them in the grass on each side of her car. I then tied thread to the knives connecting them by way of the top of her car. When she went to work the next morning, her car was in this threaded cocoon. I told her it was a gang of rogue Lilliputians; I had nothing to do with it. She was mad as hell.

Just wait until she realizes I used a case of her best sewing thread.

Ψ

Lesson Learned

1. Because nobody has been able to answer that age-old question of why there are no urinals in residential dwellings, I came up with a no muss-no fuss solution. Piss in the bathtub.

2. Profundity comes from higher up the food chain than distilled grain. It comes from movies.

3. One word. Plastics.

Fiddler Made A Goof

I did my best to warn him. I really did. I picked up the phone and dialed.

"Hey, Milan, it's Larry. This is just a quick heads up. My old lady is gonna call you and try to set you up with one of her friends. Whatever you do just say no."

"Why is your mom calling me?"

"Not my mother, you idiot. My wife."

He sighed. "Too late. She already called."

"Crap. What did you say?" I asked.

"She asked me to come over for a friendly game of co-ed poker. I told her that I would; I'm not doing anything this weekend. But, she never mentioned anything about being fixed up."

"I knew it!" I blurted out as I slapped my knee. Then I asked, "In all the years you've known us, has she ever *once* invited you over for poker? Bro, it's a setup."

Milan and I go way back. We were friends well before I met my wife. As a matter of fact, he was the only one of my friends to tell me not to go out with Miss Springer-phile. I should have listened. So, now I figured it was my turn to save him.

"What's this all about?" he asked.

"Last week she went to a revival of *Fiddler On The Roof* and now she's decided it's her life's work to pair up the village. Listen, you gotta call her and cancel."

"Why? Now, you've piqued my interest. What's this girl like?" he inquired.

"Never mind about her. Just forget about it. You don't wanna do this. Trust me."

"Come on, she can't be that bad." Then he added, "I'm kind of looking forward to it, now."

"Dude, you don't want to go near this one, ok? Please, trust me on this." I begged.

I tried to tell him to stay away, but he just wouldn't listen.

The weekend rolled around and there we were, in my apartment ready for the poker game. We had to put the leaf in the kitchen table to accommodate the guests.

There was my wife, her sister and her husband, Fly Boy, with two out of their three kids, Milan, and me. Milan's "date" hadn't arrived yet.

The doorbell rang. Milan and I looked at each other. He quickly jumped up to answer the door. "I'll get it." That wasn't *too* obvious.

As soon as he opened the door, a toddler waddled in and put his chocolate covered hands all over Milan's pant leg. The boy's squash-shaped mom walked in after him and introduced herself.

"Hi, I'm Wendy, you must be Milan. This is my little boy, Hayden."

Stunned, Milan looked at me, then at Wendy and slowly said, "Hi, uh, pleased to meet you."

Hayden ran off to play with the other kids in the living room and all the adults sat down at the kitchen table.

"Let the games begin," I said as I looked at Milan out of the corner of my eye. He was sweating.

After a good couple of hours playing poker with numerous interruptions by the kids, I was ready to call it a night. As the big winner, I said, "Well, I'm done."

Milan was the first of the group to respond. "Me, too. Uh, I have to get up early in the morning."

As I was gathering up my chips while humming *If I Were A Rich Man*, Wendy asked Milan, "We are planning a little get-together at my place next Saturday. Would you like to come?"

Before he had a chance to answer, I blurted out, "He can't. He's busy."

"What about the week after?" Wendy asked.

"Nope, he's busy then, too," I answered.

My wife glared at me like I just put catnip in her grandmother's underwear. She chimed in, "Will you let him answer for himself?"

We all looked at Milan.

"Yep, busy," he said.

"Well, Celine Dion is coming to town next month, would you like to go with me?" Wendy asked.

"Uh, sorry. I can't. I'm booked that day. I have, uh, some roofing I need to do," he answered.

Wendy thought about it for a second. Then with a puzzled look she said, "You don't even know what day she'll be here."

You can't put anything over on Tubya. Smart as a whip.

"I have all my weekends booked for months. I'm trying to fix up my house by summer. As a matter of fact, this was my last free weekend. Sorry. I would love to, but, uh, sorry." He held his palms up and shrugged his shoulders.

"Well, I'll walk you out," I said as we headed for the front door.

Once outside, I said to Milan, "I tried to tell you, but you wouldn't listen."

"Yeah. Sorry, Larry," he chuckled.

"Don't apologize to me, I'm just glad it's over." Then I asked him, "We still going to the game next Saturday?"

"You bet."

That night I really laced into my wife for trying to set them up. I knew it wouldn't work; that everyone would be uncomfortable and feelings would be hurt. She said she saw my point but I think it was a thinly veiled attempt to pacify me.

The day before the game, Milan called me and said he had to bag the game; something came up. It was really no big deal until my wife and I saw him—and the reason he blew me off—the next day at the mall, walking arm in arm.

You guessed it. Tubya.

For the rest of the day my wife kept singing, "*Matchmaker, Matchmaker, make me a match; find me a find, catch me a catch…*"

Ψ

Lesson Learned

If you ever feel the need to butt in when your better half butts in, just butt out, or you will wind up the ass. Women have been playing matchmaker for centuries, and for good reason. They have cupid's cell phone number. Even if you vehemently believe that a particular pairing will not work, cupid gets a call from the old lady, he fires his trusty bow, and love blooms. About the only thing you can do to stop the matchmaking is boycott musicals.

RUDE NUDE

I got out of the shower and was parading around the house in my birthday suit. I dripped water on the floor in every room but I didn't care. She could yell at me all she wanted about my leaving puddles on the kitchen tiles, but it was going to go in one ear and out the other. Nothing was going to bother me, for today was my favorite day of the year. It was officially the first day of football season and I was so excited. My friends were coming over to watch football all day. Yessiree. Beer, cheerleaders, pretzels, cheerleaders, pizza, cheerleaders, funny commercials, cheerleaders—all that and football, too! Nothing was going to spoil my day. Nothing at all. At least, I hoped nothing would.

I had my head in the fridge, my feet in a puddle and my butt in the air. My wife came up behind me and said, "My brother needs a place to stay for a while, so I said he could stay here."

I bolted upright and banged my head hard on the freezer door. Clutching my cranium and praying there was no laceration in my scalp, I spun around quickly and my penis knocked the already-teetering, uncovered, butter dish off the door. Instinctively I let go of my head, grabbed my crotch and banged my forehead on the egg tray at the same time the butter landed on my foot, with the dish a few inches away.

"This is better than a Chris Farley movie."

"Everyone's a comedian," I retorted as I stood there doubled over.

"What happened? Did I scare you?"

"You're damn right you scared me." I stood up slowly. "What do you mean your brother is staying with us?"

123

"Just what I said. You know he doesn't get along with Dad and he constantly fights with Mom so he is moving out."

"He should have moved out a long time ago. He was way too old to be still living at home. I can't believe your father put up with that for this long."

"Well he's got a job now and he will just stay here until he gets on his feet."

My mouth was agape. "That could take months," I cried.

I stood there for a moment and shook my head in disbelief. "No. He can't stay here. He'll never leave. I won't allow it. Sorry. Just forget it. Tell him no."

"What do you mean you won't allow it? I am not your child. This is my house just as much as it is yours, and I say he stays here. If you don't like it, that's your issue. But he is my baby brother and I am going to help him out."

"Baby is right. The guy is 32 years old and still goes to Chuck E. Cheese. No offense, but your brother ain't exactly a pillar of mental health."

"He's just had some hard times, that's all. If you can't rely on family, then whom can you rely on? He is staying here and I don't want to hear another word about it."

"Well I'm sorry, but I have rights, too. I really don't want him here. It's an extra mouth to feed and he isn't exactly a light eater."

She folded her arms. "I told you he has a job now. He can pay for his own food."

"Oh yeah? Where is he working now, NASA? He got fired from a job operating a Ferris wheel, for crying out loud."

She sighed. "He's gotten a job as a security guard in the mall. It's perfect for him. He's always liked military and law enforcement. It'll be good for him. He starts on Monday."

"Always liked military? That's a big understatement. He's been playing with GI Joes for the past 28 years. Do you remember our wedding?"

"What about our wedding?"

"He wore a freaking camouflage bowtie and cummerbund. I have the pictures to prove it. I'm telling you he's nuts." Then I added, "And he eats a lot."

She waved her hand like she was the Queen Mother. "He is staying here. As a matter of fact he will be here any minute, so get your clothes on and help him bring in his things."

"He's coming now? Right now?"

She nodded.

"But it's football day today. Everybody is coming over. Can't your brother come tomorrow?"

"No. He's coming now, and you will be nice to him. Let him watch football with you." She touched my shoulder. "Come on, it won't be that bad."

Just then the door opened and in walked her brother carrying a suitcase, in full Security Guard regalia.

"Hi," I waved. I turned to my wife. "Great, Pudgie the Rent A Pig is home. I thought you said he doesn't start work until tomorrow?"

"He does, he just likes to wear the uniform."

He came into the kitchen, dropped his bag, pointed at me and started laughing like an emphysmatic seagull.

It was then I realized I was standing there stark naked. I tried to be non-cha-lant about it, so I said, "What's so funny? Haven't you seen a naked man before?"

He stopped laughing just long enough to say, "You have butter on your wee-nie."

Ψ

Lesson Learned

You will never win any argument if you are naked and your antagonist is not. Make sure you are either both naked or both dressed because this levels the playing field. All points made while in full frontal nudity will be quickly deflated no matter how valid. And if the argument just happens to be about family, no matter how you may try to slip and slide your point in there, you must remember that blood is thicker than butter.

Don't Suet It

When the hell did she go from PHAT to FAT? PHAT—the urban-slang acronym for Pretty Hot And Tempting—went by the wayside. She was now F-A-T. She somehow managed to lose a letter and get bigger. There was no child-bearing, no steroid intake, and she didn't seem to sit on any kind of air compressor that I am aware of, yet she looked like someone yanked the ripcord of an old inflatable raft. My friends tell me that this happens a lot in relationships. The man suddenly sees his woman as FAT. The man thinks this happens overnight when, in reality, it is a gradual process that occurs over the span of, roughly, five to six months. I didn't know this, but apparently there is a medical term for this phenomenon where men, all of a sudden, see their spouse put on the poundage: PSBR—Post Super Bowl Realization. (There is already a medical term for the woman's actual unintentional weight-gain. It's called obesity.)

PSBR happens in various homes all across the country and always at the same time of year. Mid-February. We men spend the better part of autumn and the beginning of winter engrossed in that one sport that compels us to yell obscenities at the TV, relive our youth, and talk with our mouths full. I am, of course, referring to football.

The American male goes through a depression period of roughly two weeks after the end of football season. After those two weeks, he then becomes a new person. He is more aware of his surroundings, and takes time to look at the little things. A man ingests his environment as if for the first time; assessing the newness of his consciousness. Think of the caterpillar in the cocoon. At first it is curled up in a ball, then it sprouts wings. And it then emerges, fluttering around town, going from tree to tree noticing things it has never seen.

Like the size of her ass.

Cowboys have something called a hat test. If a woman is sitting on a bar stool, the cowboy will nonchalantly remove his hat and, without being seen, place the hat by the woman's posterior on the stool. If the woman's buttocks are wider than the hat, she fails the test and the cowboy then excuses himself politely. He moves on to smaller and better things.

We Yankees can do the same thing. You really don't have to use a hat, just a standard measurement or item that, put up against a woman's rear end, would tell you if you are staying the night or taking a flight. Some guys use a microwave oven. Some guys use a notched broom handle. Use whatever works for you, although I have always found it a bit awkward to unplug the microwave oven, pick it up, and put it next to a woman's ass without looking conspicuous.

Another point I would like to make is that every man's taste is different. Some men prefer small heart-shaped butts. Some men prefer a larger, more robust kind of derriere. For me, if the lady stands in front of my TV and I can still see the ESPN logo, and the remote control still works, I'm good to go.

PSBR hit me like an IRS tax levy. February rolled around and I found myself watching some stupid reality show called *American Whiner*, or something like that, when my wife steps in front of the TV. I couldn't see the program, I couldn't see the channel selector, I couldn't get the remote to work and the room went dark. I thought we were having a solar eclipse.

It was then I regrettably blurted out, "Christ, woman! When the hell did your ass get so big?" (They definitely should add this as one of the stunts on Fear Factor.)

Now, sometime ago, I was looking back on my marriage and tried to figure out where it went wrong. I didn't want to point fingers or put blame upon anyone, but objectively speaking, blurting out that question was probably a pretty big key element in the demise of my nuptials.

Trying to apologize later was for naught. "I'm sorry I said your ass is huge. I like your ass. I LOVE your ass. Always did. I never get any of it anymore, but I've always found your butt to be ass-ilicious. Oh, please don't make that hissing sound. Honey, now, come on, retract those claws and get down off of your hind legs…"

If something like this has happened to you, don't despair. With February as the month for PSBR, it isn't a coincidence that the middle of February is also Valentine's Day. If you cannot keep your PSBR under control, as most men can't, then the Powers-That-Be gave you an opportunity to atone for your sins in the form of a loving greeting card (see the chapter titled *Glibberish*), chocolate and flowers.

Please be advised that the aforementioned holiday in no way indemnifies you against penalty. You will be paying for PSBR, in one way or another, for the next six months, at which point in time, your woman's wrath will subside.

Just in time for football.

Ψ

Lesson Learned

Never, ever, tell your wife she is fat. You may wish she could double the household income as quickly as she doubled her dress size, but that won't change the fact that your teetering marriage just got the proverbial straw. Be aware of PSBR and nix the cottage cheese jokes. You can also work PSBR to your advantage: To make yourself think your wife is losing weight, just buy yourself a bigger TV. Or a bigger cowboy hat. Or a bigger microwave oven.

GliBBerish

"What's this?" she asked, holding up the Valentine's Day card I just gave her.

"It's an onion," I replied. "What does it look like?"

"Very funny, Romeo," she retorted as she put the card down on the kitchen table face down. She looked very disappointed.

"What's wrong? Don't you like the card? Don't I get some points for remembering this dumb, over-commercialized holiday?"

"The card is lovely. I'm just not sure of the sentiment behind it."

"What do you mean?"

"Forget it, Larry. Just forget it."

"No come on, tell me what's wrong. What did I do to upset you now?"

"Forget it," she said again, and walked away.

I picked up the card and reread it, but I couldn't see what was wrong with it. It took me 45 minutes to pick the damn thing out and I thought I did a good job. The card was girlie, nice, sweet, and it rhymed. I thought it was romantic without being maudlin. What was her problem?

I followed her into the living room where we sat on the couch.

"Sweetheart, I honestly don't understand why you are so put off by the card. Could you please tell me what is wrong?"

She took a deep breath. "Did you read it?"

"Yes, a few times."

"Read it again. Out loud."

I figured I would humor her to get to the bottom of this.

"Ok," I said as I opened it. "'To my wife, my friend and my soul mate. We've been through good times and bad. We've been through happy times and sad. But this much I know is true; I wouldn't want to go through any of it without you. Happy Valentine's Day.' There, what's wrong with that?"

"Keep reading."

"Keep reading what? That's it."

"No, it's not. Keep reading."

"I don't have a clue what you are talking about. Do you want me to read the copyright? What else is there?"

"What does it say after 'Happy Valentine's Day?'"

"Nothing. I just signed it. What should I be looking for?"

"You just said it."

"What?"

"You just said you signed it."

"So?" I was getting annoyed with this line of questioning. I wanted to make a motion for a mistrial.

"So read what you signed."

"I signed it 'Love, Larry.' What's wrong with that?"

"Look again, Casanova."

I opened the card. There it was, plain as day. I signed it *Love, Larry Star.*

"Oh." I was speechless.

"Did you think I didn't know who you were?" She sat there and crossed her arms.

"Sheesh. I'm really sorry, baby. I didn't mean to do it. I guess it was habit. Please don't let that spoil your mood, ok?"

I spent the better part of the night trying to mollify her.

Her birthday was a couple of months later, and I remembered the Valentine's Day fiasco. I was determined not to have that backfire on me, again.

I made reservations to her favorite restaurant for that night. I had wanted to get her the top she was talking about the few weeks leading up to her birthday, but I just didn't have the time as I was a bit swamped that day at work. I picked up a card on my way home after getting off an hour later that usual. The traffic was worse than normal, and I had to stop for gas to boot, so I arrived home about two hours later than I wanted. Needless to say we missed the dinner reservations.

I thought I would do damage control, so I put a little something in the envelope. That night I gave her the card.

"What's this?" she asked, holding up the envelope I just gave her.

"It's a shovel," I replied. "What does it look like?"

She lifted the envelope flap, opened the card, and sat there in silence.

"What's wrong?" I asked.

"Forget it, Larry. Just forget it," she said as she left the room.

I picked up the card. It was then I realized what was wrong.

I totally forgot to sign the card.

Or maybe the twenty-dollar bill that I put in there wasn't enough.

Ψ

Lesson Learned

Just remember that the fate of your relationship is in the cards.

ThOUGht FOr FOOD

Why is it that after you have been married for a few years, your wife refuses to cook for you anymore? Remember when you were first dating? She couldn't wait to make you her specialties—you know, those exotic dishes you have never tried before—like a twice-baked potato stuffed with crabmeat that you affectionately called The Fish Knish, or those corn flake breaded barbequed pork tenderloins that were just to die for.

Or when she does decide to cook, it's only for her friends and family or for some clients at a make-up swapping party. If I happened to have been in the kitchen when she was making any kind of food for them, my hands would get slapped and she told me to go to the gas station on the corner if I were hungry. Now, I don't know about the next guy, but the Texaco foot-long is not my idea of good eating. Did you ever see those things? They lie on a bed of roller bearings for twelve hours and they never, ever seem to cook; they just sweat. Mmm-mmm! There's nothing better for dinner than wet mystery meat.

I was lucky, though. My wife was the only female in her family who knew how to cook. Take her sister, for example. Her husband, Fly Boy, would complain to me all the time that his wife couldn't even make a simple hamburger. He said he used them to scrub the grill. She would nag him to take out the garbage and he would use that old line, "You cooked it, you take it out."

He was always putting her down for making lousy food by saying things like, "Look! The dog's tail ain't even wagging." But, I say, at least she tried to cook for him. My wife didn't even make the attempt. I dined in the car most nights, talking into a clown's mouth. (How that differed from staying home and talking to Officer Porky, I'm not sure.)

To be fair, I think I can probably pinpoint where it was in our marriage that she stopped cooking dinner for me.

One year, after we moved into the house we occupied until the divorce (see the chapter titled *The Very Leased*), I had the bright idea to throw an indoor beach party in the middle of winter. The idea was to meet our neighbors and invite everyone on the block. We cranked the heat up in the house to 90 degrees. We covered the floor in the basement with plastic grass matting and put up an inflatable swimming pool and fake palm trees. We had tanning lamps and beach chairs set up around the pool, and we told everyone they had to come in bathing suits, as if they were going to the beach. We also told them it was to be a potluck and everyone should bring his or her own alcohol.

We got the RSVPs and everything was good to go.

I got a list of what food people would bring to the party and went over it with my wife. She said, "You invited the Koppisches? You know I cannot stand that woman. Why did you invite them?"

"Honey, they live two houses down, we couldn't *not* invite them. Besides, I really don't think they're all that bad."

"You're just saying that because you have the hots for her."

"No, I don't have the hots for her. Yes, Cindy happens to be an attractive woman, but I don't have the hots for her. She has very nice, uh, teeth, that's all."

"It's not her teeth you'll be looking at. I can't believe she will be in my home parading around in a bikini, in front of my husband."

"We used to go to the beach all the time. Why is this any different?"

"We sat by the bathrooms."

"Look, honey, I love you. I don't want her. Tell me, why can't you stand her?"

"I just don't like her. I hear things."

"Like, what kind of things? From who?"

"From the other wives on the block. You know, girl talk."

"Until you can give me a valid reason why you don't like Cindy, we'll just drop it, ok?

Can't you just grin and bear it for one night. Please? Come on, it'll be fun."

She looked at the list again. "Cindy's bringing shrimp salad," she whined. She put the list down and cried, "I wanted to make shrimp salad."

"Honey, let her make the shrimp salad. You can make those pumpkin bread chocolate chip muffin tops that I love so much. Ok?" I touched her cheek and said it again. "Ok?"

"Ok," she pouted.

My wife was in a very depressed mood for days leading up to the party and I knew it was because Cindy would be in our house wearing barely anything. I also knew I had to do something about it otherwise my wife would make my life a living hell. Some radical maneuvers were in order.

We requested that everyone bring their dishes the afternoon of the party so we would have everything set up by evening, just in case we needed burners or crock-pots or something. I was putting the food on the tables we had set up, when I came across this huge dish of shrimp salad. Cindy's dish of shrimp salad. I placed it right next to the muffin tops. This was going to be a blast.

I grabbed some vanilla syrup and a container of salt, dumped them into the shrimp salad, and mixed it up well. This ought to make my wife feel better.

That night, I was having a grand old time, whooping it up with our neighbors. I got caught up talking sports with the guys in the pool that I almost forgot about the salad. I did take notice that Cindy wasn't there. I guess my plan worked. She must have gotten so embarrassed her shrimp salad was being spit out in every trash receptacle and toilet all over the house, that she left.

I went looking for my wife to tell her the good news. I finally found her crying in our bedroom.

"Honey, what's wrong? It can't possibly be about Cindy, she's not even here anymore." I asked.

"What do you mean anymore? She called this afternoon and said she couldn't come to the party. She had to go to work. So, I decided to make the shrimp salad."

Ψ

Lesson Learned

There's an old saying: No good deed goes unpunished. I'm not talking about what I did with the vanilla and salt. I still stand behind that and I would do it again. I'm talking about the smell in the house for the next two months because we couldn't find all the half-chewed shrimp salad people spit out.

In One Ear And Out The Udder

It was a beautiful Sunday morning in May. I was lying in bed and just opened my eyes to greet the day. The birds were chirping and the sunlight was pouring in through the bedroom blinds at just the right angle so you could see the ghost-like misty rays graze over the foot of the bed. I was really quite enamored with how utterly soothing and picturesque the bedroom looked.

I turned to gently wake my wife and show her this painting-like glow of the room. To my surprise, she was sitting up in bed staring at me with the intensity of a termite inspector on Noah's Ark.

"What's wrong, honey?" I asked.

"You know what's wrong," she sternly replied.

My mind started racing: *What did I do? Better yet, what didn't I do?*

Let's see. I took out the garbage; I filled up both vehicles; returned her curling iron to the store (why she couldn't do it is beyond me); got the dry cleaning (which is mostly her crap and her brother's damn uniforms—that I seem to keep paying for, by the way); got the coffee for the morning—wait! That was it! I forgot the half and half.

Hold on a sec. If I did forget the half and half, then she would have said something to me yesterday. No, she probably didn't know I didn't bring it unless she got out of bed to make us some coffee this morning and I didn't know it. Yeah, that must be it. She got up to make coffee. Oh, she's so considerate to make my morning coffee. How sweet is that? And here I am thinking about how she takes me for granted. What an ingrate I am. And I forgot the half and half. We could use regular milk, though. It's not that important to me get half and half. Aw, but she likes half and half. Well, I'll just get dressed really quickly and go to the store and get the ol' half and half. Besides, it's such a beautiful day and that's the least I can do for her.

I threw back the covers and she pounced, "Where do you think you're going?"

I looked at her lovingly and said, "I'm sorry I forgot the half and half. I'll just run to the store real fast."

"Sure! Anything to get out of the house! You're not going anywhere until I get some answers."

"What the hell is this all about?"

"You know exactly what I'm talking about. Who is she?"

"Who is who?"

"You know who."

"No, I don't know who. Who is who?"

"She. That's who."

"She who?"

"That's what I want to know. Who is she?"

I felt like Abbott and Costello reciting Dr. Seuss. "Look. I haven't got a damn clue as to what you are talking about. Would you care to enlighten me?"

"You are having an affair," she blurted.

"What?" I was stupefied. This was coming from way out of left field.

"You heard me," she answered. "Who is she?"

I threw my arms up. *Here we go again.* "Who is who?"

She leaned in close to me and yelled in my face, "The girl you're having an affair with!"

"I am not having an affair," I yelled back. "Where the hell did you come up with such nonsense?"

"It's not nonsense. I know you are cheating on me. I want to know who she is."

"Look, baby. I am not—I repeat—*not* cheating on you. Who the hell told you I was cheating on you?"

Then she said it. It hit me like a Roger Clemens fastball. There was nothing I could say or do. I was dealing with a mental patient.

She said: "I had a dream you cheated on me and I caught you."

Can you believe it? A freaking dream. This is just nuts. Why couldn't she dream the freaking lotto numbers? No, that would have been too easy. She had to dream I was having an affair.

Deep breath, Larry.

They say to try to make the crazy person your friend, just like they do in all the cop shows. Try to calm them down and get them to trust you. Get them to tell you things. Get them to come out of their shell so you can subdue them with a 10,000-volt stun gun.

I'll try softening my tone.

"Honey, I am not cheating on you. You are my wife and I love you," I said gingerly. "This was all a crazy dream."

It was at that point I realized I shouldn't have used the word crazy.

"I am not crazy! I caught you red handed and you have the nerve to sit there and tell me I'm crazy? You get your things and get out of this house now!"

"You want me to leave?"

"Pack a bag and get out now! I never want to see you again! How could you do this?"

Ok, she is just an irrational kook. This reminds me of the time my friend's mom went off the deep end and started feeding coffee to the cats.

"Honey, calm down," I begged. The whole thing was just so surreal. I felt like it was all, uh…well, like it was all a dream.

"Don't you Honey me! I want you out. Now."

"Look, I have no place to go. This is my home. This is our home. I love you. It was just a dream. You said so yourself. I am not cheating on you. And I don't have any plans to cheat on you. If I ever did cheat on you I would be sure to get your approval first, ok?"

She sighed and put her head on the pillow. This was the first sign of her calming down and thinking with a clear mind.

She said, "It was very real and very vivid. I saw you with that girl. I had a feeling you were cheating on me. You are always out doing things. It's like you don't want to come home."

You're damn right I'm always out doing things. It's your freaking errands I'm always running. But, I'll bite my tongue.

"Look, I promise to make it a point to be home more. I see that it must be upsetting you if you are having dreams like this. This was just a dream, though. That's all. So, can we not talk about it anymore? Let's not let it ruin our day, ok? Please?"

"Ok," she nodded.

"Look, I was going to go out and get half and half. Why don't you get dressed and come with me? It's a beautiful morning. We could take a nice slow walk to the store."

"No, it's ok. You go." She took a tissue from the nightstand and blew her nose. "I'll be ok. Just come right back, ok?"

"Ok," I said as I finished getting dressed.

That night, when I came out of the bathroom after getting ready for bed I found the bedroom door was locked.

I knocked on the door. "Honey, the door is locked."

"I know. I locked it," she said from within the bedroom.

"What do you mean?"

"You're sleeping on the couch tonight."

"What? Why?"

"You know why."

"No, honey. I don't," I said as I tried the door again.

"Yes you do."

"I can't sleep on the couch." I was fuming now. "Your brother sleeps on the couch."

"It folds out to a bed. It's big enough for both of you."

"Honey," I said through clenched teeth. "Let me in, please."

"No."

I tried the doorknob a third time. No luck. "Jesus H. Tap-dancing Christ. Just tell me what this is all about, please."

She confirmed my worst fear; fantasy feeding off of reality and vice-versa.

She calmly said, "I know you cheated on me with her when you went out for half and half this morning."

Fed up, I said, "Do me a favor and tell me her name and address so I have someplace comfortable to sleep tonight."

That little comment cost me an additional three days sleeping next to Officer Porky.

Ψ

Lesson Learned

When accusations come by way of fantasy, and she is uncertain of the validity of your infidelity, she will invariably render a test to rate your veracity. In her mind, I admitted my guilt by going out for half and half and allegedly sneaking over to my waiting mistress to tell her the jig is up. I would have saved myself a whole lot of trouble if I were selfish and just used whole milk.

centsless

"Whom did you claim as dependents?" she asked as she slammed the pen down. "There are just two of us living here. We have no children, so I'm not quite sure what you've done here." I could tell she was on the verge of exploding.

I have always hated tax time. Not because I don't like to pay (really, who does?), but because she always fought with me over it.

Every year since we've been married it has been the same old thing:

"We shouldn't owe money," she'd say.

"We should get back money," she'd say.

"You have no idea what you're doing," she'd say.

"You are putting us in a financial hole," she'd say.

"I should've never married you," she'd say.

That particular year was no different.

"Come on, Larry. Tell me why you put down five dependents on your W-4." She folded her arms. "I'm waiting."

"Well, there's you and me," I started.

"That's two," she counted. "Go on."

Beads of sweat slowly dripped down my forehead.

I felt that any minute now she was going to strap me to a chair, shine a light in my eyes, blow smoke in my face, and inform me that she had ways of making me talk.

"I'm waiting," she snapped.

"Well. There's your brother. That makes three," I answered. I was grasping at straws.

"My brother?" She let out a puff of air. That pretty much told me she wasn't buying it, but I sure as hell had better sell it.

I raised my voice. "Yes, your damn brother." Hmm, maybe I was on to something.

"He eats more than you and me combined—and I can pack it away. He never pays for anything. He doesn't pay us rent. I pay for the food for his fat face; I pay for his filthy laundry; I pay for the razor blades for his ugly mug, which by the way he goes through like they're candy. Why does he use so many damn razor blades—his face is big, but it ain't that big. Does he shave his ass? Speaking of ass, I pay for the four cases of toilet paper for his fat freaking fanny and I pay for the plumber to come and snake the toilet once a month because he clogs it with all the damn toilet paper." I was on a roll, pardon the pun.

"He uses my electricity, he uses my computer, he uses my vehicle, he uses my phone, he uses my cable, and he doesn't give this house one thin dime. No wonder he never got along with your father. He's just like him—cheap. Cheap as last year's moonshine. Well, I'll tell you right now, I am fed up. I have had it. Tomorrow morning I am going to march my butt into my boss's office and reduce my deductions. I can't keep paying for him. It's killing me. He's going to have to fend for himself. He'll have to buy all his own stuff, although I'm not sure on his salary he can afford all the freaking toilet paper he goes through in a week." I was pretty proud of myself for thinking of that. What could she have possibly said in rebuttal? Heh, heh, heh. Larry-one, Wifey-zero.

"Are you insane?" she asked. "My brother has nothing to do with us owing money again this year in taxes. I have to tell you right now, if you don't stop what you're doing I'm going to have to do something I don't want to do. I am not going to live my life this way. If you want to sink, then go ahead, but I'll be damned if you're going to take me with you."

I guess the brother angle didn't work. I'd have to try a new approach.

"Are you threatening me? You're so high and mighty. You couldn't survive without me. What are you going to do, leave me? 'Cause if you do, take that fat, camo-loving, toilet-stuffing brother of yours with you." So, there.

Then I added, "And I'm pretty much fed up with your crap, too. Go ahead. Go. See if I care. I'll be much better off. I won't have you bitching at me for every little thing. I'll finally have some peace." This didn't appear to be going very well. I should have thought of a better new approach.

She clenched her teeth. "All I am saying is, you need to get control of your finances. I manage to budget my money; you need to budget yours. I won't be dragged down with you. I'm telling you that right now."

"Look who is talking? You spend ninety bucks a month on lattes. You have a magazine fetish, and you cannot pass a make-up counter without buying something. The last time we went to the mall, you hit every cosmetics counter so fast you looked like a powdered pinball. You have more perfume than I have tools. I don't see you budgeting too well there, honey."

"The difference is, I live within my means. You don't. You spend money like you're Bill Gates. And I won't stand for it."

That made me mad. "You live within your means? You live within your means? I pay all the damn bills in this house and you pay nothing. You get to keep your paycheck for you and I get to keep none of mine for me. Why is it such a big freaking deal that I want to go out and buy a new drill or get a couple of baseball hats? Do you really think I'm blowing my paycheck on gold and diamonds?" I shook my head. "Come on, already. You can't compare the two. I can't believe you sometimes."

"You have your priorities mixed up. I believe that the good of the marriage and the family comes before anything else. You apparently don't feel that way." She continued with this argument for most of the evening.

The next morning I relented and told her I would do whatever it takes to keep our marriage together, although I still felt like she overreacted. It really wasn't as bad as she made it out to be. She totally freaked out. I, on the other hand, couldn't see the problem. We only owed three or four thousand dollars in taxes.

"So, are you willing to take a budgeting class and try to get a grip on your finances?" she asked.

"Yeah, sure. But…"

"But what?"

"I can't really afford it."

Ψ

Lesson Learned

Perspective and compromise are the key elements to a happy, long-lasting marriage. If you don't compromise and have her perspective, your marriage won't last. Either way, it'll be extremely taxing.

The Very LeaseD

My wife and I had a long discussion one weekend about what we needed to do to live peaceably together. We came away with the solution of getting a bigger place.

"A friend of a friend at work has this house for rent for only a few hundred more a month than we're paying now. I really think if we move into a house so each of us has his own space, then we will not fight as much," she proposed. "This apartment is way too small for the three of us."

"So, I guess we are taking your brother with us then?" I asked.

"You know he cannot afford to live by himself. If we get a house, at least he'll have his own room. And you can use the garage for your football gatherings, tools, or for whatever you want. This way the living room will stay clean."

The thought of my having all my stuff in one room where she will not go to nag me is like a dream come true. I feel like I just won the lottery. I stuck out my hand to my wife and said, "It's a deal."

"Good. I'll set up an appointment for next weekend so we can see it."

The prospect of getting a house turned out to be a good thing, for a little while at least. We were both so stoked to get a bigger place that we didn't argue the entire week. But, that quickly came to an end.

The following weekend rolled around and both of us were in the bathroom getting ready for our appointment. I was standing over the sink brushing my teeth.

"Could you do that in the kitchen please?" she asked me. "I still have to do my hair."

"Couldn't you wait two minutes?" I retorted as I spit out a wad of toothpaste. "And why do you have to do your hair? We're not going to a prom. Just put it in a scrunchie and let's go."

"I am not putting my hair in a scrunchie. I want this house very badly so we need to look presentable to the landlord. And you will wear something business casual, not a sweatshirt and torn jeans. Now," she sighed, "could you finish brushing your teeth somewhere else, please? I need to do my hair and make-up."

I threw my hands up in the air and bit down on the bristles of the toothbrush. "Fine," I said as I walked out of the bathroom.

I got a few feet out of the doorway, remembered the mouthwash and turned back to the bathroom to get it.

"What do you want, now?"

"I need to get the mouthwash, if you don't mind," I answered with the toothbrush still sticking out of my mouth.

"Yes, I do mind. Why do you have to do these things when you know I am trying to get ready?"

I quickly yanked the toothbrush out of my mouth and a wad of sudsy saliva dropped on her foot. *Oops.*

"What do you think you are you doing?" she shouted as she wiped her foot. "You just spit on my foot! I hope I don't have to do my toenails over again!" She threw both hands out towards me in a strangling motion. "Will you just get out?"

"I just want the damn mouthwash. Is that so terrible? Did the freaking world come to an end because you need to move three feet for two seconds? Sheesh!"

Then I added, "And why do you have to do your toenails over? Nobody will see them but you. That's totally ridiculous."

She bent down and removed the mouthwash from the vanity and slammed it down on the counter. "Here's your mouthwash. Now leave me alone to get ready."

I grabbed it and walked out muttering to myself, "Oh my God. Was that so freaking difficult?"

I went to the kitchen and looked in the sink. It was filled with pots, dishes, glasses and Tupperware containers.

I took a swig of mouthwash, gargled, and looked around for a place to spit out the effervescent, minty liquid/saliva/toothpaste combination.

Rather than spit all over the dirty dishes in the sink, I went over to the hutch where she keeps her knickknacks, grabbed her cherished gravy boat and emptied my burning mouth.

I knew if I put the gravy boat on the counter I would hear a load of crap over it, so I put it back on the shelf. I just figured I would clean it out later and went to the bedroom to get dressed.

I put on my pants and shoes and went back to the bathroom to get the deodorant. Big mistake.

As I walked through the bathroom door, I was hit with a cloud of atomized alcohol from her hairspray bottle. To this day I swear she did it on purpose. Apparently, she claims, she didn't see me.

The hairspray burned my eyes and doubled me over. I started choking and coughing.

"Could you please stay out of the bathroom until I am done? How many times do I have to tell you?" she reprimanded as she continued to spray the liquid shellac on her hair.

In between gagging and wheezing, I said, "I'm sorry, I seem to be annoying you. I didn't mean to inhale all of your hairspray before it hit your head."

"You are always under my feet and in my way. Will you please just wait until I am done? Why can't you just do that?"

I grunted as I sank to my knees and retched in the toilet.

"Why the hell do you use so much damn hairspray?" I asked her with my head halfway in the bowl. "You know, there's a permanent hole above your head. I'm afraid to smoke near you—your head would ignite."

I continued to gag and cough. Then I exclaimed, "I think I'm dying. My freaking nostrils are glued shut."

I lifted my head out of the bowl, spat, and continued, "You know, if we get this house we won't need any citronella for the yard. We'll just sit you out there on the lawn. The bugs will declare your head as a no fly zone. They'll either drop dead from breathing in alcohol or get themselves stuck in the glue on your hair. Tell me, where exactly do you buy industrial strength hairspray, Home Depot?"

"I don't need any of your rancorous comments on my hair, thank you. Just finish getting dressed and let's go see the house."

We saw the house, and loved it. The landlord took a liking to us, and six weeks later we were throwing a housewarming party at our new four-bedroom, two-bath, two-car garage leased home.

Everyone seemed to be having a good time. We had a big table set up in our dining room for all our guests and we served a roast with a whole bunch of side dishes. We literally had everything from soup to nuts.

I have to say the food was delicious; my wife outdid herself in that regard.

I remember her Grandma's words: "Darling, this gravy is so delicious. I've never tasted anything like it before. It seems to have just the slightest hint of mint."

Ψ

Lesson Learned
Dental hygiene is paramount, but sometimes it's a good thing not to floss.

What A Waist

I woke up in our new leased house one Saturday morning—my wife had already gone to a nail appointment or something (I don't know, I didn't listen)—and went to put on my favorite jeans that I hadn't worn in a while. Holy freaking Moly. I couldn't even get them past my knees. They must have shrunk.

It slowly started seeping into my thick skull that I actually had put on a few pounds. Ok, more than a few. But, I still wanted to wear my favorite pants.

I needed to figure out how to get them on without cutting them. I supposed dieting would help, but I wanted to wear my favorite pants, and I wanted to wear them right there and then.

I took them to the sink and wet the waistband. Then, I pulled and tugged and stretched the waistband with as much strength as I could gather. Satisfied that what I did helped stretch them enough so I could wear them, I tried to put them on.

After ten minutes of trying to get them over my fat ass, I decided more drastic measures were needed. I got dressed in my sweats and took the jeans to the garage.

I figured I needed some kind of tool to stretch the waistband evenly. After roughly 90 minutes of rummaging through various rusty hardware that I had lying around, I concocted a device with two large eye screws and a turnbuckle to sit inside the zipped and closed waistband. I would turn the turnbuckle with a crescent wrench and the eye screws would push out the waistband, thus stretching it more than I could possibly do by hand.

When I started doing this I noticed the eyelets starting to poke through the fabric. I didn't want to rip the jeans, so I had to figure out what else I could use to try to stretch these pants.

The thing that came to mind was a ratcheting woodworking clamp. I figured I could just invert the ratcheting end and make it into a spreader. Yeah, that would work. Unfortunately, I didn't have a ratcheting woodworking clamp, so I took the jeans, got in the truck, and went to the hardware store.

"I'm looking for a ratcheting woodworking clamp," I told the sales clerk.

"Right this way," he said. I followed him to the aisle.

He showed me the selection. I needed a larger one than the ones displayed and he informed me that the big ones came in a three-pack for $49.95.

"Sold," I said.

I paid the guy and went back home to the garage.

I removed the ratcheting woodworking clamp that I needed. Then, I had to figure out how to reverse the clamp so it would spread instead of grip.

There was a little stopper on the end of the slider that needed to be removed. How was I going to remove that? Hmm…

I got it.

I went back to the hardware store to get a small acetylene torch.

Torch, case, and cutting tip: $183.99.

Back to the garage.

I fired up the torch, cut off the end of the slider, reversed the ratchet, and basically saw spots for the rest of the day due to the fact I didn't wear any eye protection.

That was of no consequence because the ratcheting woodworking clamp, which was now Larry's Amazing Ratcheting Pants Spreader, or LARPS for short, was working like a charm.

I hosed my pants down, and used my new device on them.

When I was satisfied that the band was stretched enough, I went to put them on.

I forgot that the pants were soaked, so I did the only thing any normal person would do when they have wet clothes—I put them in the dryer.

Forty minutes later I was back at square one.

Ok, moron. Just wet the waistband this time and don't put them in the dryer.

I went through the procedure again and tried to put them on. No dice. I thought the problem might've been in the thighs. They seemed to need a little stretching, too.

Rather than buy smaller woodworking clamps, I had another idea.

I went to the nearest tire shop.

"Do you have any used inner tubes?" I asked the sales clerk.

"What size?"

"Something in a 38 regular."

He had an extremely puzzled look on his face. "Is that your tire size? Where's the vehicle?"

"I just need something to fit these pants," I said as I held them up.

After fifteen minutes of explaining, he sold me two new inner tubes for a tractor tires. I paid the man $28.53, and I was out the door.

I went home, washed the pants again, and took them to the gas station. I stuffed an inner tube down each pant leg, put a quarter in the air compressor box, and pumped up my pants with the air hose.

I was careful not to make the tubes explode for a couple of reasons. One, I didn't want to set off any car alarms. Two, I didn't want to pick chunks of rubber out of my teeth. And three, I was already blind from staring at the torch; I didn't want to be deaf, too.

So, I had my pants filled with the inflated inner tubes and I threw them in the truck. Back home I went.

With the inner tubes still inflated, I put on the LARPS and stretched the shit out of the waistband of the jeans.

Then I hung them up in the master bedroom shower, with the LARPS attached and the inflated inner tubes still inside the legs. I grabbed my wife's hair dryer and started blowing my pants dry. I was so stoked because I was very confident my contraption worked.

My wife came home from her appointment and saw me standing in the tub pointing the hairdryer to my expanded pants.

"What's that?" she asked as she pointed her glossy just-painted fingernails at my not-yet-patented device.

"That," I said with pride, "is my solution for stretching my old jeans, so I can wear them comfortably. I call it Larry's Amazing Ratcheting Pants Spreader."

She stared at me for a few seconds, with her hand still pointing at the jeans, and her mouth agape. She let out a quick breath of air, shook her head, and walked out of the bathroom.

Later on, my wife and her brother were sitting in the living room. She was reading the paper and Officer Porky was playing a Playstation game on the TV.

I went into the bathroom to get my favorite old jeans. I let the air out of the tubes, removed the LARPS, and put on the pants. They were pretty stiff but they slid on very easily. A little *too* easily, actually.

I went into the living room.

"Well, what do you think?" I asked them both as I twirled around with my arms outstretched.

Before they could answer, my pants fell halfway down.

My wife stopped laughing long enough to say, "You need to wash them and put them in the dryer so they'll shrink. And use a softener sheet."

I stood there looking at her with my pants around my knees.

I just can't win.

Ψ

Lesson Learned

Truman Capote once said, "Failure is the condiment that gives success its flavor." This is true, because the $275 I had to eat tasted like shit.

Incisor Trading

I found it quite absurd to go to a new dentist fifty-five miles away, solely based on a $20-off coupon, the promise of free x-rays for the entire family, and the picture of a mustachioed, smiling, middle-aged dentist. But, apparently, my wife had no comprehension of that formula that men use to calculate if something is actually worth doing:

(Time + Gas) Traffic = Money-Thrown-Out-The-Effin'-Window

Couple that with her being the coupon magpie that she was, she decided to book us for the cheap checkups. Our appointment was scheduled for a Saturday.

That Friday night before we went to sleep, we had the same conversation we've always had whenever we had somewhere to be the next day.

Me: "What time do we have to wake up?"

She: "What time do *I* have to wake up or what time do *you* have to wake up?"

Me: "Well, what time do we have to *be* there?"

She: "What time do *I* have to be there or what time do *you* have to be there?"

Me: "What time do *we* have to be there?"

She: "Well, what time do we have to leave?"

Me: "It depends on what time we have to be there."

She: "*I* have to be there at 2:30.

Me: "What time do *I* have to be there?"

She: "*You* have to be there at one o'clock."

Me: "So, pray tell, what time do we have to wake up?"

This usually went on for hours. But, this time I nipped it in the bud.

"You know what? Before you give me an aneurysm, just wake me up fifteen minutes before we have to leave or three hours after you wake up. Whichever comes first. Goodnight."

The next morning we spent two hours of what normally would be a one-hour drive, due to my wife's lack of interest in sports. Had she actually given a "whit"—her words—(who talks like this?) that the Yankees were in town to kick off a four-game series with a double-header, she would have made the appointment for another week, or, if she had any sanity at all, would make the appointment with a dentist who actually resided in the same zip code.

We arrived at the dentist only ten minutes late. They handed me a clipboard and rushed me to the dentist chair.

I was frustrated from the drive, I was frustrated from missing the games, I was frustrated for being late, and I was frustrated for actually having to go to the dentist—period. But, that all waned when I saw the dental assistant that was going to give me my x-rays. She was smoking hot.

I didn't mind in the least that she made my gums bleed. Just having those dainty rubberized fingers in my mouth gave me chills.

After the last little coated cardboard was removed from my jaw, she said, "Mr. Star, the doctor will be right with you after I develop these x-rays."

I sat back, relaxed, smiled, and closed my eyes.

Ok, fantasy over.

A guy, who looked an awful lot like Al Roker in a smock, awakened me.

"Hello, Mr. Star, I'm Dr. Benson. You may call me Greg."

"Well, Greg, you sure don't look like the guy in the picture on the coupon," I said.

He laughed. "That would be Dr. Rusack. This is his practice. I'm the dentist here on the weekends. I've just been going over your x-rays and I have to say that, aside from a scaling and cleaning, your teeth are in pretty good shape. No worries, but I just want to make sure."

He shoved a mirror in my mouth and probed, raked, and scratched my teeth with some sort of miniature chrome pickax.

"Just as I thought, Mr. Star. Your teeth are fine. Just make an appointment for that cleaning with the receptionist at your convenience. And, thank you for stopping by today."

I shook ole Greg's hand, went out to the waiting area, and walked over to the receptionist.

My wife got up from her chair and came over and asked, "Well, what happened?"

"Nothing. I have to make another appointment."

She gave me a smirk. "Aha! Just as I thought. Your teeth are terrible. I hope the dentist didn't pass out from your halitosis."

"You are a very funny woman," I retorted.

She folded her arms and then added another snide comment. "Tell me how many cavities you have. Two, three?"

"You take great pleasure in my pain, don't you?" I asked.

"No, it's just that I know you. You are lazy about everything else, so why wouldn't you be lazy about dental hygiene? I figured you would have a few cavities." She seemed to take pride in her assumptions.

"Well, dear, not everybody spends as much time on themselves as you do." Then I turned to the receptionist, "The doctor said I need an appointment for a cleaning."

"How about three weeks from today, will that work?" asked the receptionist.

"Gee, I don't know…" I was waffling.

"If you're worrying about the baseball traffic, don't. They're out of town that week." She smiled.

I looked at my wife out of the corner of my eye. Her face lost that condescending smirk. She seemed to be seething.

"Wonderful," I said to the receptionist. "Let's book it."

Thinking about the gorgeous dental assistant and this receptionist's awareness of baseball, I turned to my wife and exclaimed, "I love this place."

My wife seemed genuinely disappointed that there was nothing wrong with my teeth a little cleaning wouldn't cure.

Then the door opened and that hot assistant appeared holding a clipboard. "Mrs. Star? We'll see you now. Follow me."

As my eyes followed the assistant, my wife followed her, and the door shut behind them.

Later that day, on the drive home, my wife complained, "I can't believe it. You have no cavities and I have to come back for a root canal. It's not fair."

"Bummer," I said.

I reached into my shirt pocket and took out a small bag.

"Want some Skittles?"

Ψ

Lesson Learned

Sometimes she's right and you are wrong, as in the case of trying to find a new cheaper dentist. No problem there. Admit your mistake and move on. But, when she's wrong, trying to get her to admit it is like pulling teeth. The best thing to do is give her a peace offering. Like candy. Lots of sugary, chewy, stick-to-your-teeth candy. They love that.

Thar She Blows

She walked purposefully into the living room, where I was in my favorite position of lying on the couch, and exclaimed, "Ok, I've had about enough of this."

I could feel my stomach knot. Here comes another barrage of complaining. "Enough of what?" I asked.

"I was wondering how long it would take you to notice." She stood over me, tight-lipped, with her arms folded.

Was I supposed to notice something? Now I'm in trouble. "Notice what, dear?"

"That nobody has been cleaning around here. I'm so tired of you never lifting a finger to do anything around the house, so I decided to not do any more housework and see if you noticed. But I can't stand the smell anymore. Didn't you notice all the dishes piled in the sink? Most of those have food caked on so badly it'll take a year's worth of soaking to clean."

"I thought the dishwasher was broken. What do I know?"

Oh, she was really fuming now. "What do you know? What do you know? Apparently nothing. I'm running out of things to use to eat off of. I'm tired of using old Tupperware bowls to drink milk."

"So," I answered, "just do what I do and drink out of the carton."

Oops. That really ticked her off. She threw her arms up in the air, violently shook her head, and screamed. Nothing distinct, and not really a high-pitched scream, but something more with a guttural tone.

If I didn't know any better I would think she just had an orgasm. But instead, she's having a conniption. (I half expect her to run around the coffee table twitching and screaming, "Connip! Connip! Connip!") You really do have to know a woman to distinguish orgasm from conniption. Frankly, I would rather witness the orgasm. This conniption crap sucks.

Now that I thought of it, I wondered if she could have a conniption without me. Or, if there were any battery powered devices that would bring her to conniption. Or, what I would feel if I caught her connipting with someone else. Would I be jealous, or would I want to join in? I guess it was just one of those riddles that men would never solve.

"What do you want me to do?" I asked in the most soothing tone I could muster, given the circumstances.

"Do? Figure it out, Larry. I don't want you to ask me what needs to be done, I want you to take the initiative and get off of your fat, lazy ass and help me around the house with all the chores. I cannot do everything myself in this house. The garbage has been piling up for a week, but do you think to take it out? No, you don't. You are more concerned with the point spread for your stupid football games than you are with helping your wife around the house. I thought things would change when we moved into this bigger house, but apparently I was wrong. You were a fat, lazy, inconsiderate jerk then, and you're a fat, lazy, inconsiderate jerk now. I am not going to stand for it anymore. I am done with you." She stormed out of the room.

I sat up and shot back, "I am not inconsiderate!" I'll give her fat and lazy, but inconsiderate is just way out of line. Seconds later I heard the front door slam.

I took a deep breath and fell back down on the couch. I felt like I was a trailer in Louisiana the day after the hurricane hit.

I stared at the ceiling for a few minutes to collect my thoughts. Ok, it was time to assess the situation. I picked my fat, lazy ass off of the couch and went into the kitchen.

I had no idea what she was so pissed off about. No big deal. Just a few dishes in the sink.

And an overflowing garbage pail.

And crumbs and crusties all over the counter.

And papers and bills and newspapers on the kitchen table.

And mold growing in two out of three containers in the fridge.

And three day old coffee in the coffee maker.

And used paper towels in the microwave.

And mud, tomato, and soda stains on the linoleum.

And a pot on every burner on the stove, each with a different color of dried crud.

I whistled. This was awful. It was like I was seeing it for the first time. Well, I supposed I should get cracking and do something about this.

I went to the bedroom, stopped in the doorway and looked in. This room was hit hard, too. There were clothes everywhere, at least 5 different pair of shoes around the bed, and crap all over the nightstand.

This really required serious damage control, I thought. So, I got dressed, and hurried out the house to the store.

I got back home, slid everything off the kitchen table onto the floor, and put my purchase square in the center of the table. I couldn't wait for her to see it. I went back to lie down on the couch.

A few hours later she came home. She looked at the sink, the counters, the floor, and the fridge. She stood there shaking her head saying, "Nothing's changed. I can't believe nothing's changed." She then turned, walked to the bedroom and shut the door.

I guess she didn't see the flowers.

Ψ

Lesson Learned

Sometimes you can't see the forest through the trees, or in this case the flowers. There will be times in your relationship where buying her flowers will not fix the problem. You really have to sit down and ask yourself what can you do to appease her and make her life easier without compromising your principles. In this instance, instead of buying her flowers, the correct choice would have been to spring for a cleaning lady, so you can relax on the couch, ulcer-free.

Pre-Divorce Sex

[Sigh.]

Ψ

Lesson Learned

Big surprise there.

THE DIVORCE

Better a tooth out than always aching.

~ Thomas Fuller

Doctor Do Little

A few days after one of our fights—I think this one was over a spoon—I approached my wife. "I think we should talk."

"I have nothing to say," she retorted.

"Look," I said. "I made an appointment with a marriage counselor who comes highly recommended. We are headed for divorce if we don't do something."

"You can go alone," she said.

"No," I shot back. "You see the word 'marriage' next to the word 'counselor'? That's a pretty good indication that we both need to be there."

"No, I am not going. Nothing will ever change."

"Why are you so damn negative all the time?" I asked. "Apparently we cannot figure out how to live together in harmony. We need to get some help."

"I'm not paying for a marriage counselor. If you think you need a psychologist, then by all means, go to one. But, I am quite sure nothing will help you."

I was seething. "Why must you put me down constantly? This is precisely why I think we need to go to a marriage counselor. Doctor Dearmont, the therapist I made the appointment with, has excellent credentials. Baby, I can't live with the constant fighting anymore. Can't you see I am willing to try? You can at least meet me halfway, you know."

It took another couple of days but I finally managed to get her to go to one session.

The sign on the door read: D. Dearmont, Ph. D. We walked into the counselor's office and were met with an outstretched hand.

"You must be Doctor Dearmont," I asked. "It's a pleasure to meet you. I've heard nothing but good things about your practice."

"Thank you. Please, call me Diane."

I picked a female counselor figuring it would make my wife a bit more comfortable. Maybe she would open up to a female better than a male because they have that woman-bonding-collective-consciousness thing going on.

After the introductions, the doctor motioned with her hand, "Please, have a seat."

Dr. D. looked to me like a flower child of a flower child. She had a long flowing patterned skirt, and beads. Lots of beads. Beads on her neck, on her waist, on her wrists, on her ankles, in her hair—*just tons o' freaking beads*. There were beads on her wall, on her chair, on her diploma frames…Sheesh! I felt like I was sitting in a room full of polyps.

"So, tell me," she began, "what prompted you to come see me?"

Before I could speak, my lovely wife chimed up. "I didn't want to come here. He made me come here."

I was incredulous. Not to mention embarrassed. I turned toward my wife, "I *made* you come here? You said you—"

"Ok, I can see we have a lot of built up anxiety," Diane interrupted.

She turned to my wife and said in a very disarming tone, "Now, why do you feel that you don't need to speak with a relationship counselor?"

"Larry will never change," she started. "He has a problem with money. He is irresponsible, unbearable, oafish, slovenly, selfish and excessively tardy. He never does what he promises to do, never lifts a finger to help me in the house and never takes the initiative for anything. If it weren't for me, he would be out on the street living in a box."

I was fuming. "What do you mean I—?"

"Larry," Diane showed me her palm, "you will get your chance." She turned, "Please continue."

"I am sick and tired of his going out with his friends every night of the week. He always talks about his needs. What about my needs? Don't I count for something?"

Diane turned to me. "How do you feel about what she said?"

"She says I don't take initiative. Who took the initiative to come here to fix this damn marriage? Me," I tapped my chest, "that's who. She is not supportive of me at all. She knew from day one that I like to watch football. Now she does nothing but bitch and moan about my watching football. She is not supportive in any way, shape or form of anything I do."

My wife stood up. "I am not supportive? I do all the dishes, do all the laundry, do all the cleaning—how can you say I'm not supportive?"

I stood up. "You think that washing crap makes you supportive? It doesn't. It only makes stuff clean. With you, everything I do is wrong. You talk down to me, belittle me, and are verbally abusive."

"Just because I say words that are not in your vocabulary doesn't mean I am verbally abusive."

Diane stood up and tried to say something, but I continued to address my wife.

"You see? Right there is an abusive comment. It may be a backhanded comment, but it's abusive, nonetheless."

"I am just finished with you and your attitude." She turned to Diane. "There is no talking to him. He is absolutely incorrigible."

"I'm incorrigible? I'm incorrigible? I don't know what that means, but I'm sure it isn't a compliment. I haven't gotten a compliment from you in years. Instead, you just constantly browbeat me. That's what you are. A browbeater. Maybe I should call you a 'frau beater' because I feel like I live in a concentration camp. When I come home from work I never want to put the key in the door for fear of what shit I'll get from you on the other side. You let me know right away what I didn't do or what I did do. No matter what it is, I am wrong."

I turned to the good doctor. "She's not the same person anymore. She used to be fun. She used to be exciting. She used to be sexy. You know, when we were first going together, she was very meticulous about her undergarments. She used to wear sexy underwear and lingerie. Now her bra and panties don't even match."

My wife looked at Diane. "You know why they don't match? Because I actually *change* my underwear."

I looked at my wife. "Very funny. Feel free to mock me all you want. I know the truth," I said as I tapped my chest again.

She said, "Just so I am clear on this—I can feel free to mock you, correct?"

I looked down and shook my head. "I can't stand this anymore."

"Well, well, well," said my wife. "We finally agree on something. I can't stand this anymore, either."

She held out her hand and turned to Diane. "It was very nice to meet you, but I feel this marriage is not salvageable."

With that said, she turned to the door and walked out.

Diane sat back down at her beaded desk, picked up a beaded pen and said, "That'll be $100. Same time next week?"

Ψ

Lesson Learned

Here are the three things about counseling that I've always known, but to which I never really paid attention. My first eye-opening factoid: You can't spell "therapist" without spelling "the rapist." Second: Don't have your marriage hinge on a quack that you picked at random off the back page of the city's free underground newspaper. And third: Make damn sure you use separate cars to get to the appointment.

A Cold Day In Hell

Dear Satan,

I have been married to your disciple now for a few years and I feel that you and I need to talk.

I don't know what happened after we signed the marriage license but almost immediately, my life became, well, to put it quite frankly, a living hell. I was flogged with constant complaining, bemoaning, vituperation, and belittlement. I have to tell you I am at wit's end on just how to handle this.

I am in a no-win situation. If I get a divorce, I will lose all of my worldly possessions. If I stay, I will lose all of my worldly sanity. She is unwilling to cooperate on any level. This, in a nutshell, is what I am faced with.

Looking at the grand scheme of things, I realize that this is just a miniscule event in the overall structure of your operation. When you acquire new and worthy agents, such as my wife, each one must go through a rigorous training course on your business practices and corporate guidelines. And, although I never actually found the handbook, I think my wife passed your Pitchfork 101 course with a 4.0. Kudos to your scouting department on seeing the raw talent that my wife possesses.

As I go higher up your corporate ranks, I find that your pupils graduate with various degrees of Evilness. There is the associate's degree in Depravity and Maliciousness, the baccalaureate in Horror and Abomination, the master's in Atrocities, and the doctorate in Heinousness. I fully realize my wife is wet-behind-the-horns; a new-hire; a mere freshman in your organization, carrying that lone Certificate of Wickedness, but she is well on her way to upper management. You should be proud. And in an odd way, I am as well.

I know you have hunger, war and pestilence to tend to, so I'll make this brief. My soul is definitely not on the market, but I think you and I can come to an agreement as to how to handle this situation.

Here is the bottom line. I never want to see her again. I want out. I want out of this shell of a marriage. And I want out with minimal damage to my wallet, my pride and my psyche. You, my dear Mephistopheles, can make this happen. Although my soul is not for sale, I propose that you can lease it for a period of three years after I sign on the dotted line. After the three years, my soul would then revert back to my sovereignty and we can then go our separate ways. The reason I pick three years is simple. I have been a tortured soul for four years. If you add the three years, that would equate to the average seven years one would get for committing a felony. So, you   see, I consider this three-year period in your servitude to be my parole.

Mull it over, draw up the contract, and get back to me ASAP, ok?

Eternally not yours—yet,
Larry Star

Ψ

Lesson Learned

This crap never works.

campy counselor

I picked up the phone and dialed the number on the computer screen. An older female answered. "Law offices of Newman, Halderman, Erlichman, and Dean. How may I direct your call?"

I cleared my throat. "I was looking online for a divorce attorney and I came across your website, 'I-ain't-ever-gonna-see-my-shit-again-dot-com.' Is that you guys?" I asked.

"Yes, that would be us, sir. How may I direct your call?"

"Well, I need an appointment to speak with a lawyer about my divorce."

"Very well. Do you have a preference?"

"Yes. I want her to suffer."

"No, sir, I meant did you have a specific attorney with whom you would like to consult?"

She sounded like she smoked three packs a day. "No, ma'am. Uh, wait. Yes. The cheapest one."

She seemed to have dismissed my request. "Are you available tomorrow afternoon at 3:30?"

"Yes," I answered. I would have to make arrangements to get off work early.

"Excellent, sir. I just have some questions for you. May I have your name?"

I gave her all the information she asked for which seemed to have taken 45 minutes. I think I forgot to tell her my favorite color was green and I threw up on my shoes in the third grade. Oh, well. At least I got the ball rolling.

Tomorrow came around soon enough and I found myself in the waiting area of the lawyer's office staring at the Selma Diamond clone whose voice grated on me the day before. She growled at me to have a seat, that Mr. Newman would see me in a few minutes.

Mr. Newman, huh? The headliner. Wow. Pretty cool. The first guy in the title of the place. How's that for service?

A few minutes later he emerged. "Mr. Star, I presume," he came at me with an outstretched hand.

He was younger and much shorter than I expected. But, I guessed, much like shampoo, attorneys also come in trial size.

What if this guy graduated last in his class? Somebody had to be last, right?

"Follow me to my office," he said.

Then, he turned to the old lady behind the reception desk. "Have Carolyn send me those diaries and check the billing for the Gwin account."

"Yes, sir," she crowed. Boy, she sounded like she's grinding coffee beans.

"Thanks, Mom." Then to me, "This way, Mr. Star."

Mom? What's with the mom crap? We got to his office and I asked him, "Pardon my being bold, but you look a little young to be the head guy here, Mr. Newman."

"My father is the Newman on the door. He's the senior partner. I am an associate here."

"And your mom is the receptionist? How the hell does that figure?"

He emitted a grunt. "Oh, she isn't my mother," he explained. "Mom is just an endearing name we call her. She has been with us for years. She likes it and it makes her feel good."

"Oh, good, 'cause I was getting worried there for a minute. So, your website says you specialize in bitches. What do you need from me? Do you need a bitch? 'Cause I got one if you need one."

He didn't even give me a courtesy smirk. Stoic little bastard.

"Well, let me see here," he said as he opened what apparently was my file. "It says here you have no real property."

"Hey, everything I have is real," I interrupted. "It ain't much, but it's real. There's nothing imaginary about it."

"No, Mr. Star. No real estate. No real estate property."

"Oh. Uh, that's right. No property."

"And you have no children. Is that correct?"

"Yes, sir. No kids. As a matter of fact, the only Offspring I have are a few CDs that I don't want her to get her grubby hands on."

"Yes, of course," he grumbled.

I could tell that he didn't get it.

"The Offspring is a band," I explained. "I have a few of their CDs. You asked if I had children, so I said the only Offspring I have..." I left the statement hanging in the air like a fart in a humidor. He must think I'm a total schmuck.

"You've listed all your personal property, debt, income and vehicles," he said going through the papers in the file. "Do you have any investments, corporations, bonds or annuities?"

"No. Although, I should have invested in Blow-up Dolls R Us before I walked down the aisle. But, no. I had to have a wife instead. We see where that got me."

"Yes, of course."

This guy is as deadpan as they come. Have I got a girl for you.

"This is going to be a fairly simple dissolution. Is she amicable?"

"No, she's Catholic."

He held his breath for a second. Then he said, "Will she sign the divorce papers without any argument?

"Who the hell knows? She could argue with an onion. She's hot and cold. It depends on the day."

"Well, I'll have the dissolution drawn up and get it to you in a day or two. Do your best to have her sign them and then we can get our court date."

I stood up. "Thanks, Mr. Newman."

I started the door and then turned and asked, "How much is this going to cost me?"

He looked at me solemnly and said, "Don't worry. We'll let you keep your Offspring."

Ψ

Lesson Learned

Attorneys have no sense of humor.*

---

* If you happen to be a lawyer, I was only kidding about that crack that attorneys have no sense of humor. Attorneys are the funniest bunch of people I know. They're a riot at parties. Not only do they dress well, but they also have impeccable taste. And, boy, are they good-looking. Please, oh, please, don't sue me.**

** If an attorney does sue me, it only validates my previous point that attorneys have no sense of humor.

The 21 Club

Things I kept in the divorce:

1. Boxes of crap.
2. A broken computer.
3. More boxes of crap.
4. My CDs of The Offspring.
5. Even more boxes of crap.
6. Nine and a half pounds of bad mayonnaise.
7. Her bills.

Things I lost in the divorce:

1. My truck.
2. My TV.
3. My stereo.
4. My VCR.
5. My entertainment center.
6. My espresso machine.
7. My dishes.
8. My utensils.

9. My pots and pans.
10. My kitchen table.
11. My hutch.
12. My couch.
13. My coffee table.
14. My night stands.
15. My armoire.
16. My dresser.
17. My books.
18. My collection of football cards.
19. My tools.
20. My autographed baseball of the 1974 NY Mets.
21. My wife. And her freaking family.

Ψ

Lesson Learned

Chances are, if you have been through a divorce, your list would look pretty similar to mine. As much as it pisses you off, try not to dwell too much on item number 7 in the things you've kept. Instead, take a gander at item number 21 in things you've lost. Not a bad trade if you ask me.

IN THE END

Life is divided up into the horrible and the miserable. The horrible would be terminal cases, blind people, and cripples. The miserable is everyone else. When you go through life you should be thankful that you're miserable.

~Woody Allen

That Sinking Feeling

I was rummaging through the stuff she left behind under the sink in the bathroom trying to decide what was of use to me and what I would throw away.

Let's see…

Three unopened bags of cotton balls: *Nah, toss 'em.*

A Ziploc pouch of some kind of little wooden spears: *Too big for toothpicks and too small for skewers for the grill. Should I toss them? Maybe it would give me greater pleasure to use them in the fireplace. Ok, keep 'em.*

Half a dozen travel-sized little bottles filled with different color goo: *I have enough goo. I don't need more goo. Gone is the goo.*

What appeared to be six million bobby pins: *Oh, these are so gone. I couldn't begin to tell you how sick I got of finding these little suckers all over the house.*

An unused birth control pill dispenser filled with pills: *Whew! Dodged that bullet. Gone.*

A half a bottle of Nair: *Garbage. Oh, wait, that's mine.*

A new-in-the-box lighted magnifying mirror: *Hmm. Let me open this and take a look.*

Hey, check this out. It's one of those cool scissor type mirrors that mount on the wall. The kind the Three Stooges used with a boxing glove on the other end. I suppose I could use it to shave.

I looked at myself in this magnifying mirror and I didn't like what I saw. This thing magnified every little imperfection. No wonder women are self-conscious all the time. I noticed all these wrinkles I never knew I had. This thing made my crow's feet look like an aerial map of the Yangtze.

I also noticed my hairline was getting very thin. Great. I got shrubs growing on my knuckles but I can't keep a full head of hair. It was like one of those plants that you want to stop growing tall, so you pinch the top leaf and it grows fuller out the sides. Someone must have pinched my head when I wasn't looking.

This erosion of my youth really bugged me, so I held the mirror up to the other mirror on the medicine cabinet to get a better perspective on my vanishing hair. That's when I noticed that my head is actually the shape of a pterodactyl's. If I ever went completely bald it would look like I was wearing a flesh-toned bicycle helmet. I must have been a forceps baby. Now I know why, when I was growing up, all the kids called me Plunger-head.

This mirror goes in the trash. I don't need to be reminded I'm getting older. Now, back to the crap under the sink.

An opened box of super absorbent tampons: *My first impulse was to throw them away. But after thinking about it for a minute, maybe these would come in handy. They'd be great for sopping up oil spills in those hard-to-reach spaces in the engine compartment of a vehicle. Just lower one of these puppies down with the string, and faster than you could say, "I should have never married that venom-spewing, egomaniacal, fire-breathing, harpy, nagging she-devil!"—your oil spill is gone.*

Or, I could keep some with me at all times for date-emergencies. Chicks love it when a man is prepared for any situation.

Or, I could keep them in a glass on the kitchen counter as a joke, just to see if anyone notices.

Or, I could go with my first impulse and chuck 'em. Yup, I think I'll just do that.

Back to the sink.

One caked-up bottle of pink nail polish: *I can't throw this in the trash fast enough. Sheesh, I just hate that damn color. And she picked a shade that just seared my eyeballs. Good effin' riddance.*

Hmm, what's this?

One small mangled tube of Preparation H: *Ha, ha, ha! She had hemorrhoids! It's very comforting to know she wasn't lying every time she called me a pain in the ass.*

Smiling, I looked at the tube of cream and noticed it said, "New, non-greasy formula with no unpleasant scent."

Excuse me, but given the nature of the area to which you would apply this topical ointment, I don't really see how an unpleasant scent is a high priority. Ok, in the garbage you go.

I stuck my head back under the sink and found an unopened bottle of over-the-counter diet pills. Full on caffeine-laden, appetite-suppressing diet pills. It appeared to me that maybe she should have at least tried to open this bottle. Maybe she would have if they were chocolate-dipped diet pills.

Hmm, check this out—the label says, "Discontinue if sleeplessness or loss of appetite occur." Excuse my idiocy, but isn't that what it's supposed to do?

I was almost done.

An opened box of Monistat 7: *Ha, ha, ha! Apparently, she was out of whack front to back! Boy, oh, boy, don't that beat all? Funny, all the things you find out about a person just rummaging through a bathroom of leftovers. Ha, ha, ha! A vaginal infection. Serves her right, too. Ok, in the trash with you. Ha, ha, ha! I'm gonna laugh for days over this.*

Ok, last item.

One opened box of condoms: *I'm not smiling. I never saw these before.*

Ψ

Lesson Learned

Going through your ex's leftover feminine products and bathroom items is a little like cruising for chicks at a Goth-bar. You never find what you like, and you most assuredly never like what you find.

Facial Profiling

Single, again. Hmmm. I must say it felt really good. I was all alone in that big old house with no nagging, no fighting, no upset stomachs, no brother-in-law and, most of all, no wife. My money was now mine. Well, some of it was anyway. At the very least, I'd save a ton on toilet paper.

So, I thought: What should I do with my newfound freedom? After careful consideration, debating wants and desires with time and wherewithal, coupled with various other factors, I came to the conclusion that the first thing I should do is get a new chick.

This time I was going to handle the chick-acquisition a bit differently. After five years of what was virtually prison life, with a woman who didn't share any of my interests, I now knew what I really wanted from a woman in a relationship (besides sex without having to beg for it). I had a mental list of criteria that I felt she should possess and I'd make no compromise. After all, it was my life and I shouldn't settle for anything less. I will, henceforth, affectionately refer to this female-of-desire as: Ultimate Girl, or UG, for short.

Now, I am realistic about what is attractive to a woman. Chiseled looks, a hard body, a fat wallet and a fast car are things that most women look for when choosing a man. I possess all of those attributes—only in a slightly different order. I have fast looks, a fat body, a hard wallet and a chiseled car. I just needed a girl with dyslexia.

Although people might've raised some eyebrows on how I would acquire my lofty goal, I was quite certain, in this day and age, that it was attainable.

What's my method for finding Ultimate Girl, you ask? Why, the on-line personals, of course.

I was sitting at my new computer (a gift to me, from me, celebrating my singledom, while at the same time spiraling me toward bankruptcy) and it was eight o'clock on a Friday night. The first thing I needed to do was pick a site. With the myriad of dating sites scattered all over the Internet, it was a daunting task. So, I did what anyone else would do with no patience for this crap and clicked on the first one that popped up.

Next, I needed to set up a profile, which involved picking a login name. I always hated this part of registering on anything on the web because every name I would pick would either be taken already or sound too much like something out of a racing form. But, I knew this would be the first thing that women would see when they peruse my ad, so it had to be good. After all, you never get a second chance to make a first impression.

So, I spent the next two hours picking out a name from list of ten that I wrote down. When I finally went with *blueeyedhunkmuffin*, I found out it was taken. In hindsight, what girl is going to want to meet a guy who calls himself *blueeyedhunkmuffin*?

I was getting fed up with racking my brain for a login name, so I just chose *aloginname* and it worked.

I performed a search for the women in my area and read some of their profiles. A lot of them say "HWP" (which stands for Height, Weight Proportionate), "average build," or "fit," but when you look at their photos, you see they are obviously overweight. I don't get it. If you are fat, just say so. Sheesh.

A good portion of the women's profiles I looked at said they love hiking, boating and long walks on the beach. How can all these fat women do all these activities? If you ask me, they did all their hiking from the couch to the 'fridge.

It said there on the home page that ads with photos generate more hits, so I grabbed the little camera ball on top of my computer monitor and clicked away.

I took about half a dozen pictures of myself at my keyboard—some head on, some from the side and some from above. But, with the lighting and the fact that it was eleven o'clock, I looked like a character from a '50s science fiction B-movie who couldn't find the antidote. Oh well, it would have to do.

It was time to start writing my own profile. The tips section says: Write something catchy, brief and fun. Describe yourself honestly. Write about some of your likes, hobbies, etc. List the things you are looking for in a mate.

This should be quick and easy...

It was 3 a.m. I wrote that damn ad for four goddamn hours. I was so tired and my head was throbbing from thinking and writing and rewriting. It was time to go to bed, so, I just went with what I had and hoped for the best.

Here's what I posted: UG 4 UG. (Ultimate Guy for Ultimate Girl.)

Me: 40-year-old male. HWP. Likes hiking, boating, long walks on the beach.

You: Under 35. Slim. Not HWP, not Reubenesque, not curvy, just S-L-I-M, slim. Must like football, baseball, boxing, motorcycles and NASCAR. Must be ok with letting me go out with my friends. I want to be able to come home any time I please. I don't want to be nagged, yelled at, or ridiculed in any way especially in front of my friends. I don't want whining. I don't want arguments about cleaning up the damn house. I want to smoke cigars while watching TV and I don't want twenty questions if I come home late from the bar or early from work. You live your life and I'll live mine. I don't need to go out hiking, boating or walking on the beach every damn weekend. I don't even like hiking. I would rather be at the bar watching a blues band, or at the ball game rooting for my team to win without you telling me what a juvenile imbecile I look like, or that you could have married someone else and he would have made a better husband. I don't dance, never did and never will, so quit asking me to take you dancing. Get off your damn high horse and stop all your crap already! You are no prize either you know. All you do is bitch and complain about every damn little thing and I tell you I am freaking sick of it! Do you understand me? SICK!

Must like affection, snuggling on the couch, and getting foot rubs—none for me thanks. I'm ticklish.

Ψ

Lesson Learned

When writing up an appealing advertisement about yourself to capture Ultimate Girl, it's best not to do it in the middle of the night when you are punch drunk. You really do have to be honest when writing about yourself but do it with tact. You want to attract her, not repel her. But, remember not to lie because if by some miracle you do find UG, she won't stick around for long when she finds out your true colors. Then her profile will read: Ultimate Girl Left You Because U Twisted the Truth, or UGLY BUTT for short. Just don't take it personal.

Pick-up The Pieces

After around the 20th time of picking up my car-less ass to go to work and taking me home afterwards, my friend, Brandon, made me an offer.

"I know you lost your truck in the divorce, but you need a car. You have to have a vehicle. I can't keep doing this, he said.

"I know I need a vehicle, but what am I supposed to do? I haven't got a dime and my credit is shot. Paying rent on that big house doesn't help, you know."

"I know," he said as he nodded.

We sat in silence for a moment. Then he added, "You know that old beater pick-up that my father-in-law gave us a while back?"

"The one up on blocks at her dad's trailer park?" I asked.

"No, the blue one in my yard," he answered.

"Yeah, what about it?"

"Well, I was talking it over with Dawn and we decided to sell it to you for five hundred bucks. That is, if you want it."

"I'm not taking your wife's vehicle. What's she gonna use?"

"We're getting another car. With the baby coming and all, we can't use that little truck anymore."

I paused. "Let me think about it."

"You don't have to pay me all the money up front. You can give me $25 a paycheck if you want," he offered.

"Twenty-five bucks might as well be a thousand. I don't know. Let me think about it."

189

A few days later I gave him my answer. "Ok, I don't need groceries. I'll take it."

Even though there are many people who may disagree with me—like psychologists, doctors, and other quacks in the medical profession—I always thought it best to rationalize things in a positive light. Like: *I'll just have these three last drinks before I leave the party. No use in wasting good liquor.*

Or: *It's just a mole—I wouldn't worry about it if I were you.*

Or: *So what you cut off your arm with a chainsaw? At least your wife won't nag you to do the yard work.*

Such was the same with my new truck.

It was tiny—tinier than a truck had a right to be. I surmised when they washed it they threw it in the dryer instead of shaping it on a towel. But, small was good. Small was good.

It was light blue. It was a kind of Mel-Gibson's-face-in-Braveheart light blue, but at least it was blue. And, it was foreign. The truck, not Mel Gibson.

But, more important than size or color, it was, for all intents and purposes, a truck. An honest-to-goodness truck. An honest-to-goodness truck with what appeared to be horrible acne, but a truck, nonetheless. It really wasn't anything a little sandpaper, Bondo, and primer couldn't fix...on a hot summer's day...with a team of CAD designers...and a small miracle from a winged deity...

But, the best thing about it was it was all mine. No more bumming rides.

The tires were something special, too. Each tire on my new vehicle was not only a different brand, but also a different size. This was good because in case I ever get a blowout, I'd have a hell of a lot more options to choose from, as far as new tires went.

I could use any brand gas, and any grade octane. It didn't matter. And the gas mileage was great. At least I thought it was great until I realized the fuel gauge was broken.

I had to enter the vehicle from the passenger side because there was no door lock on the driver's door. There wasn't even a door handle. Actually, I think the door was welded shut at one point because they were going to enter it in the local demolition derby. The window net should have given it away.

It took about five tries in the morning to fire it up, depending on how cold it was outside. But, once that marble-in-a-blender sound died down, it was actually kind of quiet—if you could get the windows up all the way.

As soon as I drove down the street, my eyes would tear up. A few minutes later I was light-headed. It was fumes from the engine, but I figured if I could endure years of that repulsive perfume with which my ex-wife drenched herself every morning, I could endure this.

The real problem was when I put on the heater. I think I found Mengele's long lost stash of Zyklon-B pellets in the air duct. Once the heater was on, the atmosphere in the vehicle quickly turned to that of Pluto. It got all brown and cloudy in there, not at all unlike an average day in Los Angeles. I gotta tell you, if Teddy and Mary Jo were driving this vehicle in '69, they'd never have made it to the lake. They would've passed out in the parking lot.

Also, something seemed to be stopping the speedometer from going above 45 miles per hour. Brandon thought it might be a kinked speedometer cable. I thought it might be power.

All in all, I think it was a fair deal, even though I would be spending my last $50 a month for a vehicle that I was afraid may not get me to where I'd be going. Actually, it wasn't that I was afraid the car would die. I was afraid that *I* would die.

Ψ

Lesson Learned

Buying a used vehicle is a lot like marriage. You're all enamored with it those first few weeks, then you really start to see what's wrong. You could elect to get rid of it, or you could accept it and work on it, throwing good money after bad, until it chokes the life out of you.

One Man's Trash

One day, a friend of mine posed this question while hanging out on my torn, welfare sofa watching the old snowy black and white: Why the hell are you staying in this freaking house all by yourself? My answer to said friend: Uh, I dunno. Cuz I'm a schmuck?

Then, like an epiphany, the proverbial light turned on in my head. It was time to move.

It was time to rid myself of any memory of my life with my ex-wife in this house. Time to really start a new chapter in my life. Time to go apartment hunting.

I found this great deal on an apartment not far from my job. It was a two bedroom, two-bath townhouse in a pretty seedy part of town, but the rent was terrific. It was less than half of what I was paying in that house by myself over these last months. Although it was pretty tight money-wise—I would be paying rent on both places for a month—I knew moving into this apartment would really help my cash flow in the long run.

It was one of those places that was a bit weather-worn on the outside, but pretty decent on the inside…in the dark…if you squint—kind of like that fat chick you pick up in the bar at a quarter to two in the morning. And, just like that aforementioned fat chick, I care not what the place looks like just as long as it has no plumbing problems.

I had about two weeks to pack up and move. I absolutely *hate* packing and moving. Go ahead, ask any fat guy you know: What is the one thing you hate to do? He'll tell you pack up and move (some fat guys will tell you bending over to pick up the house keys they dropped is the one thing they hate to do, but for this story it's packing and moving).

I had to formulate some sort of plan. The first thing I need to do is discard anything I am not using, wearing or coveting. This includes old sweatshirts, torn underwear, broken dishes, bent utensils, charred pots and pans, the aluminum foil TV antenna, and the boxes of crap I stored in the attic.

I knew that going through those boxes was going to take a long time, so I prepared to spend the entire weekend in the dusty attic. I knew it would be bittersweet to sift through the memories of my marriage in some of those boxes, but more importantly, it would be cathartic.

I grabbed a garbage bag, rubber gloves, a flashlight and some Kleenex for possible mouse poop (I am very hantavirus-aware), and crawled up into the attic.

Box number one contained a lot of pictures of us from our dating days. I picked up an old photograph of us at the fair. Tsk, tsk, tsk, would you look at me? God, I was svelte back then. What the hell happened?

Look at her. God, she was...uh, she, um...well, let's just say she sure as hell didn't like hiking.

There must have been hundreds of photographs, but I painstakingly went through them all. I threw out all the ones of her and kept all the good ones of me. Vanity at its finest, huh? When I got to the photos of my long-lost motorcycle, I almost cried, but I quickly realized I used up the Kleenex blowing my nose from the dust.

The weekend wore on as I went through every single item in every single box. There were boxes of extension cords, television cable, telephone wire and old disposable lighters.

There were boxes of Valentine's Day cards, birthday cards and Christmas decorations. (The Christmas decorations were mostly broken ornaments from the time I knocked over the tree while trying to set up the patio furniture near the fireplace. Don't ask.)

There were appliance boxes filled with those freaking bridal magazines of hers. I felt like dumping those fuckers all over her mother's lawn.

There were boxes of her dental technician books, her massage therapy pamphlets, her veterinarian assistant forms and some pie making recipes, not to mention that unopened case of peas. *God, I hate peas.*

I spent all weekend going through all the boxes. I threw out everything of hers and mostly everything of mine. I was done. Or so I thought.

I took one last scan of the attic and that's when I saw it. There appeared to be a lone box tucked in a crawl space right under the eave.

I crawled over and reached in as far as I could, but I couldn't grab it. I had to go down and get the broom—the one with the three remaining bristles (I used some of the bristles as kindling)   to help me slide it out.

Minutes later I was on the floor of the attic with the box in my hand. I opened it and pulled out what was inside.

It was her wedding dress.

What the hell am I going to do with this?

Ψ

Lesson Learned

You never know. You just never know

CONCLUSION

About the only real advice I can give you about marriage is that nothing good has ever come from neglect. It doesn't matter what it is—food, health, transportation, urban areas, or even creativity—nothing can thrive from being left alone. *Everything* needs tending to once in a while.

So, if you're thinking of traveling the road to The Big D—and I ain't talking Dallas, you may want to remember that an ex-wife is forever. Are you sure you're ready to make such a commitment?

ACKNOWLEDGMENTS

I'll try to make this not sound like I've won the Academy Award.

Thanks to:

Brandon Hildebrand for taking care of just about everything for me, since day one. And he did it all for free. What an idiot.

Stephanie Becker and NBC's Today; MSNBC's Countdown; Toren Anderson, The Punchline Comedy Club, Austin, Cindy, Ray and the Star94 radio station in Atlanta; CNBC; KING5-TV in Seattle; In Touch magazine; Time.com, Yahoo, and Earthlink; all of the media both in the U.S. and abroad that took their time to give me time.

Comedian Tim Wilson who gave me the best advice: "If you wanna be a welder, hang out with welders. If you wanna be a comedian, hang out with comedians." I hang out with morons.

Heather Newman for her initial editing of this manuscript until she decided that giving birth was more important than me. Sheesh. Chicks.

My attorney, and close friend, Eric Newman for pretending to laugh with me and not at me.

Fellow Buzzcuts bandmate, Stuart Gordon for his strong support, network base, and wit, with whom I will be writing a cookbook. I didn't get this figure with diet and exercise, you know.

The rest of The Buzzcuts family—Carolyn, Craig, Dana and Earl—all of whom lent me money, which, to date, has not been paid back. I consider it payment-free loans. They consider it welfare.

Tom Glassman for his editing prowess. And for not vomiting.

Julie Mains. She is the best succorer on the planet. (Get your mind out of the gutter. Look it up.)

Karen Shreffler for her clerical work. And to think, she ain't even a cleric.

Wes Shreffler for his guidance and direction. Besides, he looks kind of cute in that crossing-guard uniform.

Tom C. Wilson for pointing out that a contraption much like the LARPS can be purchased from any *Harriet Carter* catalog for $4.88. We are no longer friends.

Phil Whitmarsh, Mike Altman and the crew at iUniverse. Apparently, POD will take any POS.

Alicia Love for her love, support and encouragement. Plus, she's hot.

eBay. eNuff said.

978-0-595-35692-8
0-595-35692-3

Printed in the United States
31234LVS00004B/1-33

9 780595 356928